Conquering the Iron Giant

Conquering the Iron Giant

The Life and Extreme Times of an Off-road Motorcyclist

GRAHAM JARVIS

WEIDENFELD & NICOLSON

First published in Great Britain in 2019 by Weidenfeld & Nicolson
an imprint of The Orion Publishing Group Ltd
Carmelite House, 50 Victoria Embankment
London EC4Y 0DZ

An Hachette UK Company

1 3 5 7 9 10 8 6 4 2

A CIP catalogue record for this book is
available from the British Library.

ISBN HB 978 1 4746 12845
ISBN eBook 978 1 4746 12869

Typeset by Input Data Services Ltd, Somerset

Printed and bound in Great Britain by Clays Ltd, Elcograf S.p.A.

MIX
Paper from
responsible sources
FSC® C104740
FSC
www.fsc.org

www.weidenfeldandnicolson.co.uk

For Jack and Ellie

Acknowledgements

I would like to thank the following people for helping me make this book a reality: James Hogg, Paul Murphy, Tim Bates, Lucinda McNeile, Alan Samson and John Hulme from *Trial Magazine UK*.

I'd also like to say a massive thank you to my girlfriend Sandra for jogging my memory and to Mum and Dad for the stories and photos.

Author's Note

Those who know me will probably be surprised that I've written a book. Actually, that's an understatement. I'm known for doing most of my talking on a motorcycle, and I have to admit that when the idea was first suggested to me I was a bit taken aback. There's only one thing I hate more than talking and that's talking about myself so my initial answer to the question, *would you like to write an autobiography*, had to be, No. No Way!

Then, a few days later, the publishers came back to me.

'But you'll only have to talk to one person,' they said. 'He'll help you write the book.'

I still wasn't convinced.

If you search for 'Graham Jarvis' in YouTube literally hundreds of videos will come up; anything from GoPro videos I've done during Hard Enduro races such as the Erzberg or Romaniacs or clips from early Trials to me coming a cropper or doing a circular wheelie on a mountain. Search for 'Graham Jarvis interview' in YouTube, however, and you'll get two: one I did for a German website which lasts a few minutes and in which I say almost nothing, and a profile that Transworld Sport did on me in 2012 in which I say – almost nothing.

It didn't bode well.

In the end, and after a bit of toing and froing, I managed to find my voice and the process has been very enjoyable, not least because it's brought back so many memories. It's funny the things you remember once you start talking and because I've been doing this a while now there's been no shortage of stories. Not all are repeatable but the ones that are have been included in this book.

1

Unusually for a participant in motorsport, as far as I know I don't have a single trace of it in my family background. Amateur or professional. I get my competitive side from my grandad who did a bit of boxing but to the best of my knowledge that's about it for sport. My dad worked for a printing company for twenty-five years and my mum was a home help so unless they've been keeping something from me about one of my relatives or were masquerading as a motorbike-and-sidecar team at the weekends, I can state quite categorically that I am the first person from my lot to do anything even remotely spectacular on either two or four wheels.

My first ever bike was found in the woods behind our house, in a place called Sturry, in Kent. Sturry is about three miles outside Canterbury and the most interesting fact I can tell you about the town, which I nicked off Wikipedia, is that Orlando Bloom went to one of the local schools. I bet he never won *Junior Kickstart*, though!

I was born on 21 April 1975 and about four years after that my dad walked through the back door one day carrying something that looked suspiciously like a child's bicycle (although

I've recently realised after looking at a photograph that it was a girl's bicycle!).

'Look what I found,' he said.

'Whose is that, Cliff?' asked Mum.

'Nobody's, I think. I found it abandoned in the woods. It's a bit rusty and hasn't got any brakes but it'll do for Graham.'

Yeah, who needs brakes?

The wooded area Dad was referring to was like an adventure playground and it's where all the kids from my area went after school and at weekends. From the age of about four until I was fifteen I must have spent 90 per cent of my spare time there and the majority of my memories involve me riding either a bike or a motorbike.

I can remember feeling excited when I got that first bike but I don't remember riding it. According to my dad and my brother Barry, the first thing I did when I got my hands on it was to start popping wheelies. At that age, wheelies were normally pulled with both feet on the ground but according to them I was riding along on my back wheel after just a couple of days. That's been my trademark for as long as I can remember so now you know why. It obviously came naturally.

My next bike, which I got when I was about six, was a different kettle of fish and I was virtually glued to the seat for as long as I had it. Believe it or not my dad found this one at a tip (times were hard in those days) and although I don't remember the name of the bike it had big wheels and thin tyres. This was before BMXs arrived in our area. The reason they're significant is because road tyres enabled me to do skids and in 1970s and 1980s Britain, young lads were judged by one of two things: how far you could wheelie, or how far you could skid. As somebody who had already mastered the art of wheelieing, this just left skidding, and without wanting to blow my own trumpet, although I will, I was rather good, even at that age.

One of the reasons I couldn't do wheelies was because the bike was twice the size of me and was probably meant for a ten-year-old or young teenager. I didn't mind, though. Pulling a skid on that thing was incredible.

Despite having a brother called Barry who is five years older than me and a sister called Rita who is seven years older, I think this was when my parents began to discover the true financial cost of bringing up children, as I tended to go through rear tyres like monkeys do bananas, and tyres weren't cheap in those days. Come to think of it, they're not that cheap now.

My passion for skidding was inspired by regular trips to the local speedway track, which was my first introduction to motorsport. The team was the Canterbury Crusaders, who are no longer in existence, and they raced at the Kingsmead stadium. The Crusaders were quite a big team in their day and had won the national championship back in 1978.

Although the early 1980s wasn't quite the golden age of speedway, it was still a lot more popular than it is today and the riders were big stars. Bruce Penhall, Hans Nielsen and Simon Wigg were just some of the names I remember from that period and they were what inspired me to try and bankrupt my parents. I must have been doing quite a good job in that department, as instead of paying to watch the speedway like everyone else we would sometimes sneak through a hole in the fence. As well as being quite exciting, it meant Dad had more money for tyres, so it was all good. It didn't stop at speedway, though. If we ever went anywhere as a family, say to a safari park or somewhere, at least one of us would have to hide under a rug in the back.

One thing I remember about going to the Speedway was the atmosphere. I have no idea how many people used to go – a few thousand, maybe – but to a young lad of seven or eight it seemed like millions. It's also quite a noisy sport, which obviously added to it, and I remember some of the language was quite colourful. Riders often pull wheelies at the start of speedway races (although they're not always deliberate) and I remember seeing one rider fall flat on his arse when this happened and the entire stadium started laughing. It didn't put me off wheelies, though.

While we're here I suppose I'd better give school a mention, although it'll be quick.

Basically, I hated it. Not disliked it. I really hated it. I wasn't what you'd call sociable, but as well as having no interest whatsoever in any of the subjects I just wanted to be out on my bike. The worst part was going back to school after the summer holidays. If I were a betting man I'd say that a lot of people reading this will know exactly what I mean. It used to kick in about a week before the holiday ended. Either my mum or somebody else's would say something like, 'You'll be going back to school in a week', and the moment they said that a cloud would start to descend over my world. A cloud that said goodbye to fun and hello to boredom.

My entire life revolved around playing outdoors on my bike and if I wasn't doing that I wasn't happy. That's no exaggeration. It's what I lived for. Dad used to come and meet me from school sometimes and he could never understand why I was always the first pupil out of the doors. And I was always the first pupil. Without fail. Looking back, I think it was because I was the one who wanted to be there the least, and I made a fine art of making a quick escape. The trick was to always make sure you were at the back of the classroom for the final lesson of the day, and, most importantly, were ready to do a runner the moment the bell went. Most pupils used to spend a few minutes getting their stuff together and chatting after the bell rang, by which time I was already half-way home. The swathe of relief that used to sweep over me when the bell went was incredible. Like winning a really tight race. The dawn of BMX had arrived and Father Christmas had bought me and my brother a bike each. The skills and challenges were endless.

There was a gang of us who all had bikes and everyone was the same. You might watch a bit of telly every so often but the majority of the time if you weren't either at school, sleeping or having your tea you were out riding.

By far the biggest thing to happen in the whole of Kent in the early 1980s – at least in my life – was the opening of a new BMX track in Herne Bay. With grandad's competitive nature obviously coming to the fore, I asked my dad if he'd enter me for a race. Fortunately he said yes and after arriving at the track I started messing around on one of the ramps and trying to do a few tricks. You're probably expecting me to say that this was where I got the Trials bug, but it wasn't. It didn't matter, though. I was there to race, and the only thing I could think about, even then, was coming first. If you ask my parents or my brother and sister what I was like as a child, apart from claiming I was quiet, which I was, they'd probably say something like, 'He always had to win, did Graham!' I think my brother Barry experienced this more than most as we used to play together a lot, and I have a sneaking suspicion that I might just have got on his nerves occasionally as my desire to win was bordering on the obsessional. It's obviously part of my DNA so you could say that winning was my first ambition.

Funnily enough (although it's hardly surprising), the only time I used to talk a lot as a child was after a Trial and Dad reckons that we could travel all the way up to Scarborough and I wouldn't say a single word, whereas on the way back, providing I did well, I wouldn't shut up! As an incentive, Dad used to say that if I did well at a Trial we could stop off at a Little Chef restaurant on the way home and I could order anything I wanted from the menu. As somebody who likes grub almost as much as he likes winning, this was the perfect motivation for me and it used to cost Dad a fortune.

I don't remember feeling especially nervous as I lined up at the start of that BMX race. We'd made our own track in the woods at home and despite the difference in conditions I was already an old hand when it came to BMX racing. In fact, the only thing I hadn't experienced yet during one of our races – I'd already won, lost and fallen off – was a blowout. Unfortunately that's exactly what happened on the first corner in the first race at Herne Bay. Ten seconds in, and – BANG!

The only plus side was that I managed to stay on and because it was unexpected and very, very loud I made half the adults watching almost crap themselves. It wasn't much of a consolation, but it was better than nothing. At least they'd remember me!

I didn't go back for some reason, so that was both the beginning and end of my BMX career. I think my dad tried

8

to persuade me to go back, but as well as being a bit embarrassed I realised that I wasn't that interested in racing. At least not unless it was in the woods with my friends. By this time I'd also started doing back-hops, which was like discovering skidding all over again. The only part of school I could stomach was the dinner break as that was when me and my mates would compare numbers. I wish I could remember how many I used to be able to do but I was definitely one of the better ones.

From the age of about nine to ten I was a member of a gang. Some people who know me probably won't believe it, but it's true. The rest of the gang were all older than me, and you could say that I'd just fallen into bad company. I don't remember duffing up any old ladies or anything, but as well as smoking, which made me sick, we used to hang around on street corners and try to look menacing. That was quite difficult for me, because as well as it not being in my nature to be menacing, I was the most innocent-looking child you could ever meet and wasn't capable of knocking the skin off a rice pudding let alone beating somebody up or terrorising pensioners. The first time I took a puff on a cigarette I didn't inhale and thought, *This is good. How cool am I?* The second time I'm afraid I did inhale, and about five seconds later I threw up all over my mate's trainers. Being the one who'd told me to inhale he didn't have a leg to stand on, or should I say a trainer to stand on, but I didn't half make a mess of them. You won't be surprised to learn that it put me off smoking for good.

The only reason I became a member of that gang in the first place was because I looked so innocent. Every time they wanted some cigarettes, I'd be the one to go to the shop (I said they were for my mum) and every time I went to buy them, I'd get served. In that respect I was invaluable. But, in the end, being in a gang didn't suit me one bit, so I soon gave up my life of crime.

Once I was back to being a normal kid again, I was able to resume my career as a BMX trickster par excellence. Having mastered the back hop, me and my mates decided to make things a little bit more interesting.

'Why don't we make a ramp and then jump through fire?' one of us suggested.

At first there was silence as nobody was quite sure if they were being serious.

'How do you mean?' one of us said.

'I've seen it on telly. Some stunt men built a great big fire underneath the end of the ramp and then jumped through it on their bikes.'

'What if we fall off into the fire?' one of us asked.

Silence.

'We could always make it a small fire?' somebody suggested.

'Yeah, go on then!'

Fortunately, there was a lot of natural banking in the woods as it was an old sand quarry, so it provided us with a lot of ready-made jumps. Instead of going to the trouble of having to make a ramp for our 'stunt' we just built a fire at the end of one of those. If memory serves me correctly, we had a hell of a job getting the fire started, so in the end we forgot about the dangerous bit and just carried on jumping. It was probably for the best.

The largest bank in the woods was situated right at the end of the old sand quarry and was called the end bank. As well as being very steep (it was almost vertical in parts), it cut away at the bottom into a stream that used to dry up a lot, and only the very bravest would attempt to ride down it. By the time I plucked up the courage to give it a go I was almost a teenager, and, as far as I know, nobody had ever cleared it before. At least not in my lifetime. In fact, just a few days before my attempt a lad had knocked himself out while attempting to descend the bank and he was the latest in a long line of injured riders.

When I finally took the plunge it felt like the most natural thing in the world, and after clearing the stream I remember feeling quite chuffed with myself. The end bank was legendary to us lot (it was our Everest!) so being the first to clear it on a bike was a big achievement.

For a few hours every weekend the woods would be transformed from a playground, in which kids rode bikes and didn't light fires, despite their best efforts, into a free-for-all for road bikes, scooters, and everything in between. Kent was a bit of a hotbed for Trials in those days, and the best riders in our area were three brothers called Morphett. Steve, Phil and Kevin. They were the opposite to me in that they came from a motorsport background, and I think they had the dubious honour of being the first people I admired on two wheels apart from the speedway riders. As well as brand new bikes they had all the rest of the gear and the thing I remember most about watching them ride is that they made it look so easy. I used to stand there watching them thinking, *I want to do that!*

There was another rider called Brian Dobin who also came riding. He cleared areas and made us sections using twigs for markers (sections are basically the obstacles and areas over which Trials riders are judged), so although it was only a practice it was all done properly. He used to ride a bit too, did Brian, but he wasn't very good. Sorry Brian! He was so enthusiastic, though, and as soon as he started building the sections I'd run over and help him. I found that bit fascinating, and fortunately he could see how enthusiastic we all were and explained what he was doing every step of the way. This meant that before I'd even ridden a Trials bike, thanks to Brian Dobin I had a little bit of knowledge about how it all worked. Once the motorbikes had gone we'd ride the sections on our push bikes for the rest of the weekend and after school the following week. We also used to score ourselves, so to all intents and purposes we were doing everything the Trials riders were doing, just without engines and helmets – and to a much lower standard!

What made it exciting, and what I grew to appreciate, was that instead of watching professionals on telly or at an event, which is what most people had to do if they wanted to see their sporting heroes, I could watch them every weekend and free of charge practically in my own back garden.

To be honest, I don't think I'd even heard of Trials before they started practising there, but after just a few weeks I was itching to get on a motorbike and have a go. For those of you who come from an Enduro background or are completely new to Trials like I was, allow me to give you a quick, and hopefully non-patronising, heads-up. Basically, Trials – sometimes referred to as observed Trials – is a non-speed motorsport using specialised motorcycles and the idea is to clear various obstacles, which are in sections, without putting your feet down, falling off or stopping dead. In every section you're scored by an observer, hence the name observed Trials, and every time you touch the ground or an obstacle with your foot you're given a penalty point. There's obviously a lot more to it than that, but that's it in a nutshell.

Riding Trials felt like a natural progression from what we'd been doing on our bikes. Not just on the sections, which we used to ride after the motorbikes had gone, but everything else such as negotiating rocks and flying over homemade ramps. A motorbike, though? Getting my hands on one of those would be the best thing ever, and the more I watched the Morphett brothers and all the other riders the more I wanted one. It was just before my tenth birthday and it was time to start pestering my dad.

Before I could do that Brian Dobin took my brother Barry to compete at a Trial. He'd got into it a few months before me but unfortunately he was about as good as Brian was. I'm close to Barry, so I can say that. He wasn't the best. He's clever though, as is my sister, so they definitely got all the brains.

Because my dad had just bought my brother a motorbike, he couldn't really say no to me. We had actually talked about me doing grass track or speedway at one point, but when the Trials boys started practising in the woods that went out of the window. I think he managed to fob me off for about a week, but in the end resistance was futile. I am joking, by the way. My parents have always moved heaven and earth to encourage me, and if that's what my dad had had to do to get me a motorbike, he'd have done it. He knew how enthusiastic I was, and as he'd watched us in the woods I think he also had an inkling that I might be quite good at it. Good at it or not, I just wanted a bloody motorbike!

A few months earlier, when my brother had started competing, Dad had bought a Nissan Cabstar, which is a type of pick-up truck. After leaving the printing world, he'd started working with my uncle Ron, who ran serviced petrol stations, so he used it day-to-day. He also bought a trailer that would go on the back of the car, so we had enough gear to get five bikes to a Trial, let alone one. Or two, as it would soon be.

We eventually settled on a second-hand TY80, which Dad bought for about £300 from a man who lived in Watford called Michael Guy. Believe it or not, Michael's now the sports editor at *Motorcycle News* and he's even written the odd piece about me over the years. It's a small world. Fortunately for Dad, that was the first and last motorbike he ever had to buy me so I wasn't as expensive as I could have been.

The TY80, or the Yammy 80, as it was also known, was the standard entry-level bike for Trials and it was what I'd been hoping for. Even as a child, I wasn't what you'd call the most excitable human being on earth and would take things like Christmas and birthdays in my stride. 'Yep. That's nice,' I'd say after opening my presents. 'Thanks very much.' There was no whooping or leaping around the room. That's just not me. This was different, though, and although I didn't start jumping about when Dad told me he'd found a bike, I did feel a twinge of excitement and asked him if we could get it immediately. Unfortunately, it was near London, and we could only collect it the following weekend. I think it was Sunday when he told me, so I had to wait a whole five days. Add in a week at school, and it was the longest five days in the history of the world. It was torture!

The bike was in really good condition and when I first saw it my stomach started doing somersaults. I loved my BMX and carried on riding it, but this was a new challenge. Incidentally, there was a trick I used to pull on my BMX that used to have my dad scratching his head and because he couldn't figure out how I did it I used to do it all the time. We had a wall at the end of our front garden that was the width of a brick and I used to ride to the end of the wall, spin my bike around in mid-air, and then ride it back again. It's quite a rudimentary trick by today's standards but Dad used to love it. He was always a very appreciative spectator.

Like the bike, my helmet and gloves were also second hand and for the first couple of years I wore jeans while competing. There's a photograph of me doing my first Trial in jeans somewhere and I was even wearing them when I entered my first national up north. I wasn't bothered, though. I had a bike and that was the main thing.

One of the first things I started doing once I got my bike, apart from tearing up the woods behind home, was pulling the odd wheelie. As I said earlier, my second bike was too big for me to pull wheelies on, but the TY80 was smaller, *and* it had an engine. About five days after we got the bike, I pulled a wheelie in the woods, but unfortunately I went too high, looped out and ended up smashing my mudguard. As you can imagine, I was in no hurry to show the bike to my dad and it was about half an hour before I plucked up the courage to take it home. In the end he was OK about the mudguard.

'I'm more worried about the bent forks,' he said.

'What!?'

I was absolutely gutted. I had no idea I'd bent the forks.

'Don't worry. I can fix it. We just need a new mudguard.'

What a relief!

Despite being a former member of a notorious gang, I was quite well behaved most of the time, so when I did mess up it was usually OK. I wasn't always like that, though. I used to be a right little sod when I was very young, and one of my earliest memories is throwing things at my mum from the top of the stairs mid-tantrum. Who'd have thought it? I soon grew out of it (although I'm still prone to throwing the odd tantrum every now and then). Mum wouldn't take that crap for long.

The first time I ever competed on a motorbike was in a Trial at a place called Invicta Barracks, which is an old army barracks near Maidstone.

It was a standard club Trial, and I was entered in the beginner category. The only thing I remember about the Trial is being let off by the observer on the first section. It wasn't especially challenging, but because I hadn't walked it properly beforehand, I missed where the end card was, and when I stopped at what I thought was the end of the section some of the spectators started shouting at me. 'Keep going!' they said. 'That's not the end.' I'd obviously put my foot down momentarily, but because I was a beginner – and because I probably looked like I was about to crap myself – the observer just smiled, waved me on and gave me a 3 instead of a 5.

One of the next Trials I entered was an indoor event that took place at an equestrian centre. According to my dad who filmed the Trial, the announcer – a man called Ron Stephens who was also the chairman of KYTC (Kent Youth Trials Club) which we belonged to – was quite impressed by my ability to scale cars, and during his commentary he said, 'Here's young Graham Jarvis. Look at that, he's only been doing it a couple of weeks. Surely he must be a star of the future?'

The results for club Trials were always sent out the following Monday and would almost always arrive on the Tuesday.

I remember the first time as if it were yesterday, and because our post usually arrived before I went to school I was able to open the envelope as soon as it arrived. I remember sitting with my bowl of cornflakes by the front window and when the postman came into view I ran out of the house and virtually mugged him. 'Can I have our post please,' I said. 'Can I?' God knows what the postman must have thought, but from then on it became a regular thing and if he hadn't arrived by the time I had to go to school I'd go looking for him! Every Tuesday, providing there'd been a Trial, I would accost him and demand our post – politely. Tuesday became like Christmas to me, and it would have been the same for thousands of other kids all over the country. You didn't always get the result you'd been hoping for, but nobody could take away the excitement you felt prior to opening the envelope.

That first one was particularly special, as I'd won the category.

'Mum, Dad, I won. I won the beginners' class.'

I probably said it in a very matter-of-fact kind of way, but really I was on the verge of exploding.

Winning the beginner category meant that for the next Trial I went straight into C-Class, which is the category for eight-to-twelve-year-olds. I had a competitive streak right from the start, as I remember feeling a tremendous surge of nervous energy before travelling to the Trial and then again before competing. That kind of experience is part and parcel of being a competitive human being, and despite finding it slightly unnerving early on, it very soon became part of who I am. I think if you asked any professional sportsperson what they experience before travelling to an event and before competing, they'd describe a variation of that feeling.

I said earlier that Kent was a bit of a hotbed for Trials back in the 1980s, and KYTC was thriving. There must have been at least a hundred riders in the club, so when you included all the wives, husbands and parents who used to tag along you had the makings of quite a busy social scene. The club arranged something virtually every week, but in addition to that there were two or three other Trials within an hour of us. It kind of engulfed us as a family, and within just a few months of me starting to compete in Trials we'd become part of the scene. The thing is, I think all of us really enjoyed it. Mum and Dad made loads of friends, and so did my brother, sister and I. It sounds a bit cheesy, I suppose, but it was like being part of a really big family, and when I said that Trials engulfed our family, I wasn't overstating it. It's what we all lived for. I think you have versions of this in most motor-sports. On four wheels it's usually karting from a beginner's point of view and on two wheels it's usually Trials, moto-cross, speedway, grasstrack or Enduro.

When I started competing in C-Class, I was one of the youngest in the group. In fact, the majority of my competitors were about a year older than me. This was good in a way, as it made me improve quicker and was almost like a sink-or-swim situation. It may sound a bit big headed but had my competitors been the same age as me I think I might have won most of the rounds and as well as lulling me into a false sense of security, it would have hindered my progress. As it was, I was up against a group of lads who were older and more experienced than I was, and all I wanted to do was get to their level. I managed to achieve this after about three months, and the knowledge that I'd managed to do so gave me an awful lot of confidence. Even at that young age I think

I was adamant that I wanted to be a Trials rider when I grew up, and with no outside distractions in my life – school continued to be a non-event, and girls were still terrifying – I was able to give that ambition my full attention.

2

If you regularly finished in the top three in C-Class in the South East Centre Trials Championship, which I did, you qualified for an annual competition called the Inter Centre Team Trial. In 1986 the Trial was held in Settle in North Yorkshire, and the evening before the first day we all drove up there and checked into a B&B. Well, me and my mum and dad did. My brother and sister were virtually adults by then, and I'm sure the thought of having to spend long hours in the car just so they could watch their annoying little brother riding a motorbike in a field full of farmers would have gone down like a lead balloon.

Because of the length of the drive, I had plenty of time to contemplate what might happen at the Trial, and the nervous energy I felt once I started thinking about it was incredible. Overwhelming, almost. Had the drive been an hour or so, which is what it usually was when I was going to a club Trial, it would have been fine. Unfortunately, this was more like ten hours, so by the time we got to the B&B I was exhausted. Next time, I thought to myself, only start thinking about it when you're nearly there.

The biggest difference between competing at club level in Kent and national level up north, apart from the overall standard, were rocks. I'm not sure why, but we didn't seem to have many of them in Kent, and the sections we rode at club Trials seemed to feature mud, logs and tree roots more than anything else. Yorkshire, on the other hand, is full of rocks, and one of the reasons I got myself into such a flap in the car was because I'd never ridden over them before. Although I was kind of looking forward to it, I was also worried. We'd been told to use Michelin tyres on rocks as opposed to the Pirellis that I was used to, so that just added to my anxiety. In some ways it felt like I was travelling to a different country.

The northern contingent were, on the whole, very friendly and welcoming, and the only thing that separated us, apart from the accent and an ability not to spend brass, was that half of us were good at riding through mud and over logs, and the other half were good at riding over rocks and up becks. I did feel like I needed an interpreter once or twice. Up there in Settle they speak proper Yorkshire, and if you're not used to it (I'm still not 'fluent', even though I live in Yorkshire, although I'm known to throw in the odd 'aye up' or 'nowt' occasionally), it can take you by surprise.

Unfortunately, I can't remember where I finished in this Trial, but I didn't disgrace myself. In fact, because it was so at odds with what I'd been used to, I'd say I did quite well. Again, had I done really well I might have come away believing that I'd mastered rocks and become complacent. I think I finished mid-table, so overall it wasn't a bad start, either to my experiences on rocks, the nationals, or meeting people from Yorkshire.

The sport was advancing and riders were starting to stop

and hop, as it's known, while riding a section and also roll back. It's fair to say that this revolutionised the sport and fortunately for me I'd already been stopping and hopping on my BMX for years, especially when riding the sections in the woods. The vast majority of young riders were in exactly the same boat as me, so it didn't really give me an advantage. What it did do, though, was make the sport a lot more exciting both for the rider and the spectator, as it added a new dimension and made each section more challenging. I had to learn a few new skills, but it made things a lot more interesting.

In 1987 the Folkestone Motorcycle Club, a Trials club that had adults as well as children riding for it, organised a trip to Belgium to watch a round of the outdoor world championship. The event was being held at a place called Bilstain Park, which is famous for hosting Trials. As soon as I heard about the trip, I started badgering my dad. It turned out he was as keen as I was and said yes almost immediately.

The most famous part of Bilstain Park in terms of Trials is the Bilstain step, a huge slippery rock face that put the fear of God into most riders and was considered to be almost impossible to scale. That was one of the main talking points as we made the journey over to Belgium, and I couldn't wait to see it. Back then we didn't have things like YouTube, of course, and with competitive Trials not being shown on telly a great deal it was all left to your imagination. These days the Bilstain step is actually small compared to a lot of obstacles on the world stage, but back then it was, and had been, the nemesis of generations of Trials riders, and I couldn't wait to see the sport's current biggest names try and tackle it.

One of the best things about Trials from a spectator's point of view, and especially a kid who's a member of a club and thinks about nothing else, is the fact that you can get very close to your heroes. This actually worked against me when I became a professional rider for reasons I'll come to later, but as a young spectator it was the best thing ever. The riders I was looking forward to seeing the most were Thierry Michaud, who'd already won the world championship twice and would win it again in 1988, Eddy Lejeune, who'd won the world championship three times, and Steve Saunders. In terms of heroes my choice had now graduated from the Morphett brothers to Steve. For those of you who aren't familiar with Mr Saunders, Steve dominated the British Trials scene during the 1980s and very early 1990s and as well as finishing third and second in the world championship, which he did in 1985 and 1986 respectively, he also won the British championship no fewer than ten times. He was, and is, an absolute legend of the sport and little did I know that in a few years' time I'd be competing against him. That was a bit weird when it happened!

But it was a twenty-year-old Spaniard who ended up stealing all the headlines that year, somebody who would dominate the sport for the next ten years. Jordi Tarrés was his name and, despite this being only his third world championship round, he was already taking the sport to a completely different level and his technique was just incredible. Watching somebody so young do so well was in itself quite inspiring to me and because he was only eight years older than I was he made success seem more attainable. These days we don't know how lucky we are, because regardless of which sport you follow the chances are there'll be a channel or a website that covers it. Back then, if you couldn't go and watch your heroes on a regular basis, which I couldn't, you had two options: *Motorcycle News*, which came out on a Wednesday (I think it still does) and *Motocross Magazine*, which came out on a Friday. That was the extent of our exposure to the wider world of Trials, but we used to love it. The best thing about *Motorcycle News* was that it printed the results from all the club Trials and the nationals, and if you ever got your name in, it was a big thing. That was the first thing I always did when it arrived, and if my name was in there, I'd be happy for the rest of the day. I never told anybody at school. That wasn't my way. I'd just sit there daydreaming about riding and looking at a picture of Jordi Tarrés on the cover of my schoolbook.

Actually, there was one other way we used to enjoy Trials. Every so often a video would start doing the rounds that was a recording of one of the world rounds and sometimes – just sometimes – I'd manage to borrow a copy from somebody. The quality was invariably dreadful, because as well as being copies, they'd all been watched countless times. They were treated almost like contraband in a way – forbidden goods that had to be passed on under darkness – and I'll never forget the feeling when I managed to get hold of one. It's ironic really, but the most memorable of these videos didn't feature a single Trials rider; it featured a stunt rider from France called Jean-Pierre Goy. These days Jean-Pierre works mainly in the film industry and has appeared in dozens of films, including *Skyfall*, *Tomorrow Never Dies* and *Batman: The Dark Knight*, but back then he used to do tricks and things, and I must have watched his video hundreds of times. The video featured tricks on pushbikes as well as motorbikes, and one of the things I used to try and perfect myself was the slow wheelie – something I'd been playing with since the age of about four. Eric made this look easy, but of course it wasn't. As I said earlier, that's almost become my calling card, and whenever I do Hard Enduro schools, which basically involves me travelling the world and teaching groups of enthusiasts how to ride, it's the first thing people ask me to do. I do them on a motorbike these days, but I learned how to do the trick on a girl's bike and at the age of four!

There are two other things from 1987 that I should tell you about. First, I managed to win the C-Class at my club. It was just two years since I'd got my TY80, so I allowed myself to get quite pleased about that, although you'd never have known. The main reason for this was the fact that I had to go to a presentation. They had one every year, and regardless of whether or not you'd won most of the club turned up. I was not in the least looking forward to this year's presentation, and although it didn't exactly spoil it for me, I could have done without it. I didn't like adulation and certainly not from a room full of people.

The other important event was me getting my first sponsor. It's hard to overestimate the importance of sponsorship in niche sports like Trials, so when the owner of Rex Autos, who owned a garage close to where I lived, approached me and offered me a jacket to wear with their logo and my name on it, I really thought I'd arrived. I was still wearing jeans and a second-hand helmet at the time, but at least I had a good jacket. I think I also put a sticker on my bike, so it was a big deal. I'm surprised I didn't have a manager . . .

In all seriousness, getting a sponsor gave me a huge boost, and although I already had ambitions to ride a motorbike for a living, this made it just that little bit more attainable. I was really starting to believe it could happen.

The jacket sponsorship with Rex Autos was followed soon after by an offer of a motorbike. A Honda TLM50, to be exact. I think my dad had been under the impression that the £300 he'd spent on my TY80 was just the tip of the iceberg, so when I'd been offered a bike he was happier than I was. The man who made the offer was called Roy Francis, and he ran a company called Paul Smart Motorcycles. I don't think they're in existence anymore, but Paul Smart had been quite a successful Grand Prix rider in the 1970s and had opened up a dealership after retiring. Roy had taken it over, and after seeing me ride at a Trial one day he came and had a word. Finding Roy, or should I say Roy finding me, was a massive piece of luck and he couldn't do enough for us. He was just what we needed.

Subsequently, this seemed to move me up a level, and in addition to competing a lot further afield I started riding on a Saturday *and* a Sunday. It's funny but I became so consumed by Trials that I don't really remember anything else from that period. My attitude to school hadn't changed, so there wasn't much to block out in that department, but even stuff at home is a bit vague. All I cared about was riding my motorbike or my BMX, and I would grab every opportunity I got to do so with both hands. I didn't even need asking. Just point me and my dad in the direction of the Trial and we'd be there. No problem.

The icing on the cake with regards to me attracting some early sponsorship came from the Folkestone Motorcycle

Club, who, after deciding to sell the clubhouse, decided to invest some of what they'd made from it in me as everyone involved in the club seemed to think that I had a bright future. As gestures go, it was pretty monumental and over several years they ended up giving me about £5,000, which was a heck of a lot of money back then. I was a lucky lad and I owe everyone who was involved with that club a great deal.

I suppose the biggest dream I had at the time, as it would have been for any young sports fan, was to compete either against or with my heroes, and in 1988 this actually came to pass. Well, almost. I forget when it happened exactly, but I was asked via my club if I'd like to take part in a pro-am competition on television. It was part of a programme called *Kick Start*. Those of you who remember it will already be humming the ridiculously catchy theme tune.

Kick Start was a televised Trials competition that ran on the BBC from 1979 until 1988. It was devised by the same man who created *Top Gear*, and the sections for the early shows were designed by the legendary Sammy Miller, who in the 1950s and 1960s was probably Britain's most famous off-road motorcyclist. *Kick Start* was so successful that in 1980 the BBC decided to create a children's version of the programme and so *Junior Kick Start* was born. Apart from Trials and Hard Enduro, *Junior Kick Start* is probably what I'm most famous for, and it's certainly the thing that prompts the most questions. It was presented by a man called Peter Purves, who also used to present a television programme called *Blue Peter*, and whenever people find out I appeared on *Junior Kick Start* the first thing they always ask is, 'What was Peter Purves like?' I suppose you could describe the show as a cult hit, in that it's still talked about a great deal after all these years, and if you look on YouTube you'll find dozens of clips from the show, including one or two from the episode I'm about to tell you about. If you have never seen it before, be careful of the theme tune. I warn you, you'll be humming it for weeks!

I remember receiving the letter confirming that I'd been chosen to appear. It was about three pages long, and the first thing I realised after reading it was that in order to appear on the show I'd have to have two days off school. TWO DAYS! Without further ado I asked my mum to write a letter for me to hand in to my form teacher. Actually, I think I almost threw it at her!

'What's this, Graham?' my teacher asked.

I didn't say a word. I just stood there smiling.

I'll never forget the look on her face as she started to read it. The letter must have said something like, *I'm afraid Graham won't be in on these days as he'll be appearing on a television show*, and as she read it her eyes started widening.

'Ooh,' she said. 'Fancy that!'

I think I was the first rider from my area to get picked to go on either *Kick Start* or its junior version, so it was quite a big thing really. As far as I know the reason I got picked was because of my performances in the nationals, which are the next step up from club Trials and take place all over the country. The competition is obviously a lot stiffer at these events and the sections are more difficult.

I'd finished third overall in the nationals that year, which was probably a consequence of having sponsorship and riding further afield, which did me the power of good. Either way, I had two days off school – and £50 expenses. I'd almost forgotten about that. To a young lad like me that was the adult equivalent of about £1,000 and was the other part of the letter that had made the biggest impression on me. When my dad said I could keep the money I was over the moon as it must have cost him a fortune getting me there and back.

'You're the one who's earning it,' he said. 'It's yours.'

As I just said, that was a fortune to a young lad. This *Junior Kick Start* thing just got better and better!

The pro-am was staged in a place called Easton Neston which is in Northamptonshire, and when we turned up on the first morning I remember my stomach lurching when I saw the television cameras. It might sound strange, but I hadn't watched either version of *Kick Start* very much (I was always out riding), so I don't think it had really dawned on me what I was letting myself in for. The television cameras and lighting wagons brought everything to life, though, and I think I went from being very quiet, which was and still is my default position, to being virtually mute.

The 'pros' in pro-am were all adult professional riders and the 'ams' were kids, of which I was obviously one. There were six pairs all together, and the man I was paired with was a Swedish rider called Ulf Lundquist. Nope. I'm afraid I'd never heard of him either. The most famous adult riders in the competition were Steve Saunders, John Lampkin, who is Dougie Lampkin's uncle and once finished fourth in the world championship, and the late Diego Bosis, who had finished second in the 1987 world championship and would do the same again in 1990. When it came to the youngsters, the only one apart from me who went on to become a Hard Enduro rider was Dan Hemingway.

The conditions on the day were absolutely awful, and although it didn't rain during the competition it was as muddy as hell. Normally this would have suited me, but in a new venue and with cameras everywhere it's safe to say I lost a little bit of confidence. Worse still, I was first to go, or Ulf and I were, although this could work in our favour, as the course would undoubtedly become more treacherous as the day went on.

There were six obstacles in all, and because it was television I thought you might get more than one go. 'Nope,' said the man who was looking after us. 'You can obviously walk the course beforehand, but if you make a hash of it, you make a hash of it.' That made me feel miles better . . .

On the few occasions I had watched either *Kick Start* or *Junior Kick Start* I'd seen plenty of disasters. One incident in particular springs to mind. I think this has become quite famous now – on YouTube, at least – but a lad called Mark Schofield crashed during one of the rounds, and when the two St John's Ambulance men went to attend to him, they both ended up falling arse over tit and were accused, although just in jest, of being drunk. Just before Mark sets off on his round, Peter Purves says that he must be pretty fearful after what the previous competitors did to the course, and twenty seconds later he crashes! It's one of those clips that gets played again and again. It never ages.

A few seconds before I set off, the sun came out. It was a day too late, but I was glad it made an appearance. I crossed the line in 1 minute 20 seconds, with just one 20-second penalty to add. That was actually OK given the circumstances, and when Ulf set off for his round after I'd completed the course, I got more than a bit of my confidence back. Unfortunately, this was short-lived, as Ulf fell off even before he'd even got to the first obstacle. To be fair, I think his bike just slipped on the mud, but when I saw it happen I remember thinking to myself, *why couldn't I have Steve Saunders?* Sorry, Ulf.

Fortunately my Swedish teammate managed to redeem himself by putting in a good round, and our total time including penalties (Ulf got one too which made just two between us) was 3 minutes and 26 seconds. In the end we were beaten by a young lad called Andrew Johnson, who was paired with Diego Bosis, but second wasn't bad. The best thing about the day, apart from the money and the time off school, was beating Steve Saunders, who had been paired with a lad called Andrew Holdsworth. That was an amazing feeling, as he was still one of my heroes (Steve, not Andrew), although I stopped short of talking to him or asking him for an autograph. I'd have had to be drunk to do that, but I was only twelve.

When the episode was finally aired, I got quite excited, although it did worry me slightly what the reaction at school might be. I suppose the majority of kids would have shouted it from the roof tops if they were going to be on television, but I didn't. In fact, I didn't say a word to anyone. Luckily for me the only people who saw it were the kids who had motorbikes, and apart from asking me a few questions about Steve Saunders, which I couldn't answer, they didn't seem that bothered. Had I come first it might have been different, but you know what they say, nobody remembers second place. Thank God!

The following year, having managed to maintain my position at the nationals, I was invited to make my second appearance on *Junior Kick Start*. Once again, a letter arrived confirming everything and after asking Dad if I could keep the money, which he said I could, I handed Mum a pen and paper and pleaded with her to write the all-important letter.

When I gave it in to my form teacher, I got the same reaction as last time. I just had to pray that she didn't do something stupid like remember to watch it!

To cut a long story short, I ended up reaching the final of *Junior Kick Start 1989* by winning a series of heats, and the lads I had to beat were Mark Weightman, Gareth Thomas, Andrew Johnson, Ian Needham and an up-and-coming Yorkshire rider called Douglas Lampkin who, so I was told, was tipped for great things.

Although it was a bit muddy, the conditions were a hell of a lot better than the last time, and despite going out fourth I wasn't too worried about the course. In fact, I remember feeling quite calm in the minutes leading up to my round and actually looking forward to it. Then, when the lad who went before me, Gareth Thomas, got to the very last obstacle everything changed. Dougie was leading at the time, having put in a round of 1.36 with no penalties, and because Gareth probably wasn't the fastest rider in the final the pressure was obviously on. The very last obstacle was a thin beam that went over some water, and unfortunately for Gareth he mis-judged his entry onto the beam and ended up getting wet. Once again the St John's Ambulance men were there in sec-onds but managed to remain upright this time. The accident looked a lot worse than it was, which was a relief, and Gareth managed to get back on and complete the round. His time wasn't good, though, so Dougie was still the lad to beat.

Until Gareth fell I was entirely focused on beating Dougie's time, but watching him fall off had broken my concentration a bit and had dented my confidence. All I could think about now was what could go wrong and every obstacle had become my enemy. This is when nerves will either make you or break you, and I had to try and forget about what had happened to Gareth and make my nervous energy – of which there was a lot at the time – work for me. In the end I managed it. I just brought my attention back to the here and now, concentrated on my round and took it one obstacle at a time. Unfortunately this would become harder as I got older.

I managed to complete the course in 1.34.9, a couple of seconds ahead of Dougie. By the end of the first round Andrew Johnson had sandwiched himself between Dougie and me with a time of 1.36.6. There was still a round to go, though, in which we had to ride the course in reverse.

On the second round I went out last, and when the flag went down the only thing standing between me and the Junior Kick Start Trophy was Master Lampkin, who'd posted a total time of 3.20.6. Once again, I tried not to think about what Dougie had done and just concentrated on my ride. Looking back, I realise the television cameras brought a whole new level of pressure, but they also brought a new level of excitement. I may not have wanted the adulation or even the recognition, but I did enjoy appearing on *Junior Kick Start* for the simple reason that it was something a bit different. And because I got to meet Peter Purves.

I ended up winning by just over a second and had I known how close it would be during the round I'd probably have cocked it up. Watching it back is quite nerve-racking and Peter Purves actually gets pretty excited! Dougie must have been gutted, but he'd end up getting his revenge.

When I watched the episode back a couple of weeks ago there was a bit during my second round when Peter Purves says, 'He looks good this lad [referring to me]. He comes from Canterbury and is very quiet. He laughs a lot but he doesn't talk a lot.' That kind of sums me up really, so it was very astute of my mate Peter, who, incidentally, was a very nice bloke. Just in case you were wondering.

The trophy, which was an actual kick-start mounted on a plinth, was presented to me by the marketing manager of Norwich Union Insurance. I only know that now because of watching the episode again, but when he handed the trophy to me I remember thinking, *What the hell do I do now?* In the end I just stood there and smiled. If they thought I was going to lift it above my head and shout, 'Get in there', they were going to be very disappointed. In fact, the closest I came to celebrating was when I lifted the trophy up to face height and then smiled again. That's your lot, I'm afraid! There was no prize money, by the way, as they weren't allowed to give prize money to children in those days. More's the pity.

Unfortunately, when the episode was shown on television it felt like the entire bloody school watched it, and when I went in the following day I was the centre of attention. As somebody who has probably been shy from birth this was my worst nightmare and until now I'd always managed to remain quite anonymous at school. In fact, there were probably pupils and teachers who never even knew I existed! Then, all of a sudden, I'm a flaming celebrity. The reactions to the win were quite varied, and for every person who said they were impressed by what they'd seen, there were one or two who said I was a prat. I suppose they must have been jealous, but there was no need to be. After all, all I'd done was win a kick-start on a plinth! Maybe it was the two days off school and the fifty quid?

The worst part of the day was when my form teacher got up and announced to the entire class what had happened.

'OK, everyone,' she said. 'I don't know if you all saw it, but yesterday Graham was on television, weren't you, Graham?'

I remember thinking to myself, *Oh my God. Please make her stop!*

'Yes Miss,' I said humbly.

'And what did you win?'

'*Junior Kick Start*, Miss.'

'How exciting! Now then, Graham. Would you like to come up and tell us all about it, please?'

'No, Miss.'

She obviously didn't know me as well as she thought she did.

'Really? Oh, come on, Graham. I'm sure everyone would love to know.'

The only way to stop this was to fall silent, so that's exactly what I did. The teacher soon became bored of asking, and within a day or two everyone at school had forgotten about it, just as I'd hoped. I think the people who were most impressed by me winning *Junior Kick Start*, apart from my family, were the members of the Folkestone Motorcycle Club and the Kent Youth Trials Club, but because they knew what I was like nobody made a fuss.

I had the honour of winning the very last series of *Junior Kick Start* in 1992, which took my tally to three, having also won in 1990. I think Dougie came second again in 1992. To be fair, I had a year on him age-wise, but he'd certainly improved.

When I came to write this chapter I remembered that my parents had recorded every episode I appeared in on video but when I went to watch them I realised that they no longer had a video player! Who does these days? Subsequently, I've had to rely on memory and YouTube.

My television career actually started a couple of years before *Kick Start*. In fact, by the time I first appeared on *Junior Kick Start* I was an old hand. The first appearance I made was on a programme called *Number 73*. Those who are my age or above might remember it, but it was one of those Saturday morning shows that lasted a couple of hours and featured lots of different guests. A few of us from our club were asked to appear and because it was broadcast live and quite early in the morning we got to stay in a hotel the night before. That was amazing! Our appearance consisted of us riding around an outdoor set at a television studio on our motorbikes but I can't remember why we were there and we were only on for a few seconds. The thing I remember most about the day was meeting the actress Letitia Dean who was appearing on *EastEnders*. She was a guest on the show and gave us all a signed photo. I've still got mine somewhere.

Following on from that, we were then asked to appear on a programme called *Going Live*, which is a bit less embarrassing than *Number 73*. That was huge in the mid-1980s and starred Phillip Schofield, and Sarah Greene. On the episode I appeared in the main guests were a pop group called 5-Star, who were a bit rubbish, and a bloke called Roy Castle. Roy, who presented a show called *Record Breakers*, which you won't be surprised to read featured people attempting to break world records, was appearing because of a world record attempt and I'm pretty sure that was why we were there too. I think somebody was trying to balance on a motorbike or something. The episode became famous when one of the callers who was ringing in to speak to 5-Star started using the f-word and calling them all the names under the sun. That's the bit I remember most! Again, we were just there to ride around, and although it was a bigger show we were only on for a few seconds.

At some point in the 1980s I also appeared on the local news with the aforementioned Steve Saunders. Because I was supposed to be an up-and-coming Trials rider they asked me on, and to make the piece more interesting they decided to invite an established rider. Lucky old Steve. He must have been chuffed to bits when he got the call. He was about as animated as I was, so it was a short interview. Imagine us as a double-act!

3

The Honda TLM50 that I told you about earlier was rubbish at first as it was lacking in power. In an attempt to make the TLM50 more powerful Roy Francis ended up sending it, at his own expense, to Stan Stephens who's a very famous tuner. Stan managed to get it up to about 80cc, and he even developed a version of the bike that was water-cooled, which takes a hell of a lot of work.

After taking the bike back we heard that somebody had managed to get their TLM50 up to 100cc. Not to be out-done, Roy sent it back to Stan again to see what he could do. A week or so later we went back to collect the bike and Stan said to Roy and Dad, 'It'll either go, or it'll blow up.' Luck-ily for us it went, and as far as I know it's still in existence somewhere.

I ended up winning C-Class on the TLM50, but our partnership with the bike and with Honda ended soon after that as when I moved up to B-Class it was too small and the only Honda available was too heavy and so not competitive. Fortunately, Roy set about doing a separate deal with Fantic which was extremely generous of him. I think Paul Smart was actually an exclusive Honda dealership at the time, so it was a big gesture.

I suppose one of the reasons Roy kept on helping me, in addition to me being commercial gold and an international television superstar, was because I was still progressing in Trials. As well as doing well in the nationals, I'd become B-Class champion, which is for twelve- to fourteen-year-olds, in 1989, and A-Class champion, which is for fifteen- and sixteen-year-olds, in 1990 and again in 1991, so I was still fulfilling all that early promise. Also, from about the age of thirteen, a gap had begun to form between me and the other riders, and I was winning fairly easily. I was also taking the fitness side a bit more seriously, and was acting and thinking like a professional, even though I was more or less still a kid. Or at least how I thought a professional would act. Until then my entire fitness regime had been based around my journey to and from school. It was about three or four miles in all, and I used to walk there slowly, and then run back like the wind. My mum used to despair at the expense as every month I'd need a new pair of shoes. Taking my fitness more seriously gave me another advantage, because as far as I know I was the only young rider in the country, apart from perhaps Dougie, who was concentrating on things like fitness and diet to any degree. From the rest of the country's point of view, Dougie and I were the riders to beat, and from Dougie's point of view, I was the rider to beat. I was his nemesis, I suppose, and it was my job to try and stay ahead. In fact, Dougie's progress was probably one of the things that pushed me into taking it so seriously, and while I obviously can't speak for Dougie, I'd say it was probably my progress that motivated Dougie to improve too. Had either of us not been around, then whoever was left would have won everything quite easily, and I can't say for sure that I would have been quite as professional had it been just me.

The only time I ever really socialised with Dougie in those early days was at the YMSA (Youth Motorcycling Sporting Association) Six Days Trial, which used to take place in the Matlock area and at six different locations. It was a really big event back then, and everybody used to come with their families and make a holiday of it. The atmosphere was brilliant, even to a quiet lad like me, and everybody seemed to know each other. The only holiday we ever had that wasn't Trials-related – that I can remember, at least – was when we went to Butlins but once I started riding we stopped going.

In terms of learning how to ride Trials, the YMSA was one of the most beneficial events I took part in as a child. It was always professionally run, and because of the sheer length of the event, not to mention the difficulty of the Trials, it was easily the most challenging. It was the one I looked forward to the most as a kid, and I think a lot of people were the same.

Other than Roy Francis, the person who helped me the most in those early days with regards to sponsorship was a man called Roy Carey who was the importer for Fantic. He'd been a business associate of Roy's for some time, and he ended up investing a lot of time and money in my progression.

When I was about fifteen, Roy Carey took me and two other riders to a training school in the south of France, which was incredibly generous of him. The other two riders were Steve Colley, who you'll hear a lot more about later, and a lad called Andrew Phillips. I don't remember being homesick or anything when we went over there. I was just excited. Roy drove us all down, and because we arrived late at night we had to sleep in the car. I remember waking up, and the first thing I saw when I looked out of the window was a beach and the Mediterranean. I'd obviously seen a beach before, but what I hadn't seen much of at that age were topless women. That morning they seemed to be everywhere. I remember thinking, *I could get used to this. Welcome to France!* We ended up spending the first half of the day on the beach, which was very pleasant, and then after lunch we drove up to the school in the mountains. Roy dropped us off, and then I'm pretty sure he drove on to the Fantic factory, which is in Italy. The course lasted a week, and the man who instructed us was a world championship competitor who usually finished mid-table called Gabino Renales. World Champion Thierry Michaud was also teaching that week, but unfortunately we never got him. Gabino was great, though, and once I'd managed to stop thinking about the beach he set about improving our technique. The thing I remember most about that week, was being terrified of the dogs out there. We'd been told that all the dogs in France had rabies and whenever we saw one we crapped ourselves.

'There's a dog, quick, run!'

Although we got on quite well in France, Steve Colley went on to become the only Trials rider I ever had what you might call a rivalry with. Or at least a serious one. The reason we didn't fall out over there is because Steve's a bit older than I am, and we'd never had to compete against each other. But when we were adults, everything changed. Steve is a massive character, and quite loud and outgoing, whereas I'm obviously not. He used to mouth off quite a bit both before and after Trials, and he would try and embarrass me in front of other people. Because I was very quiet, I think he thought he could intimidate me, so I generally avoided him, although there was always a mutual respect between us. I suppose the intimidation worked to a certain extent, as it sent me even further into my shell, but it never affected my performances. In fact, it probably had the opposite effect, as the only way I could get one over on Steve was by beating him on a bike.

In 1990 Roy organised another trip, this time to Finland, Germany, Switzerland and Italy. The other two riders this time were Gary Marshman, who I believe is still riding but who never went professional, and Stefan Merriman, who would go on to win the world Enduro championship four times. The part of the trip I remember most is being in Finland, partly because of the terrain, which was different to anything I'd ever ridden before, but also because we got to watch a round of the world championship. Jordi Tarrés was the reigning champion and still the man to beat. The man closest to him was Diego Bosis, who had won the pro-am I appeared in on *Kick Start*. After the Trial, Stefan and Gary, who are a bit older than me, got to ride the course, the lucky devils! After that we went to Germany where we watched the next round before travelling to Switzerland and then Italy. In Italy we got to visit the Fantic factory, which was fascinating, because instead of it just being an assembly line they actually made their own parts. They even had their own foundry where the engines were cast. We ended up spending an entire day there and were made to feel very welcome.

Another highlight from this period was training with the great Mick Andrews, who won the European Trials Championship in 1971 and 1972 (the competition eventually became the world championship in 1975 when America got involved) and is a five-time winner of the Scottish Six Days Trial. He's basically Trials royalty, so receiving tuition from someone like that was a big opportunity and a massive thrill. Dad used to drive me up to Mick's place in Buxton a couple of times a year, and after setting off at the crack of dawn I'd get to spend a good few hours with him. The hardest part for Dad wasn't driving us there and back, it was getting me off my bike at the end of the day! It was the worst feeling ever when he said it was time to go. Anyone could go, by the way. You just had to ring up and book, and because there were plenty of rocks up there the environment was spot on.

It's hard to overestimate the importance of something like this, and although it's not exclusive to Trials there aren't many sports where you can ring up one of the best in the business and book your son in for some training. Can you imagine doing that in football or Formula 1? 'Is that Lewis Hamilton? I'd like to book young Oliver in for tomorrow afternoon. Usual rates?'

The fact is Mick Andrews had been one of the best Trials riders in the world, so in real terms it was actually no different from an F1 fan being taught by Damon Hill or Lewis Hamilton. That's Trials, though. It's community driven, and everybody wants what's best for the sport.

Mick was also working for the ACU (Auto-Cycle Union) as a youth coach at the time and, as well as teaching me and lots of the other top youths in the country to ride Trials, he also guided us on things like diet and fitness, and made sure that the stuff we'd been doing at home and off our own backs was worthwhile. Fortunately it was, pretty much, and once he'd refined everything I was able to concentrate on riding and nothing else.

I remember one day Mick coming down to do a Trials

school for the Kent Youth team, which I was part of, and during the school, which took place in the grounds of a local gun club, he decided we were going to ride up a large bank. Mick went first but unfortunately he only got halfway so he tried again. 'Nope, it's no good,' he said. 'Graham, why don't you have a go?'

Just like Mick, I tried once and failed, but on my second attempt I made it. I could tell Mick was flabbergasted but with a load of kids to contend with he carried on teaching. After the school had ended Mick said, 'Right then. I'm going to scale that bank if it's the last thing I do,' and off he went to try. He made it, although it took him a couple of go's. The man's an absolute legend.

Back at home, I continued to practise in the woods as often as possible, either on my BMX during the week, which was permissible, as it didn't make a noise, or on my motorbike at weekends. Unfortunately, the latter came to a halt one day after complaints were made by dog-walkers and local residents about the noise and mess we were making. To be fair, it probably wasn't the best place to have Trials bikes flying all over the shop. Then again, the dog walkers didn't always clean up after their pets, so we weren't the only ones making a mess!

Some of the culprits had been caught and stopped by the police before, but never me. Then, one Sunday afternoon, the police turned up again when a few of us were out on our bikes, and after ticking us off they took us home to our parents. Until then I don't think I'd ever been in trouble before – certainly not with the police – and when the policeman knocked on our front door with me standing at his side, I was absolutely gutted as I'd lost my training area.

Fortunately for me the policeman was quite understanding and seemed to appreciate the fact that far from just tearing up the woods for the hell of it we were actually practising a sport. Even so, I got a proper dressing down and was told that if we got caught again within the week, the consequences would be severe. I had absolutely no idea what that actually meant, but I had no intention of finding out. To be fair to the policeman, instead of telling us to stop for good he told us to just leave it for a couple of months and then go back every so often. Apparently, he'd been watching us for about fifteen minutes before taking us home and had been impressed by what he'd seen.

Before we move on to adulthood, I'd just like to tell you about my encounter with the careers advisor at school. As you already know, if I hadn't had to go to school then I wouldn't have and in my eyes my interview with the careers advisor was simply another fifteen minutes when I wasn't riding a bike.

'So Graham,' said the careers advisor. 'What are you going to do when you leave school?'

'I'm going to be a professional Trials rider.'

This did not impress my inquisitor one little bit, and without even asking whether my answer had been based on anything other than a dream he sat up.

'You're going to have to pull your head out of the clouds young man,' he said. 'People like you do not become professional sportspeople.'

I didn't say anything. I just smiled.

Ross Noble used this story when he was narrating a film I made a few years ago called *Erzberg the Hard Way*, but instead of saying I just smiled he said something along the lines of, 'Graham said nothing as he didn't speak until he was thirty-two years old!'

That made me laugh.

It's probably fair to say that the success I had as a youngster worked against me when I started competing as an adult when I was seventeen, and I don't mind admitting that I found the transition very hard indeed. Had Dougie not been around in those early years it would probably have been worse, but the lack of competition in the youth ranks, coupled with the fact that for years I'd been tipped as being the next big thing, did me no favours whatsoever. I found the pressure, which had been building up for years, especially hard to handle. The more I won, the more people wrote and talked about me, and the more people wrote and talked about me, which I didn't like anyway, the more certain they became that one day I would win the world championship. I certainly hadn't become complacent. Anything but. I just wasn't ready for it – any of it: the pressure, the step up in ability. It was intimidating at first and then demoralising, as I seemed to have stopped progressing. My temperament, too, was probably at odds with what was needed at the adult level in that I was a bit of a shrinking violet, and even my fitness, which I'd always taken seriously, was found to be seriously lacking.

In hindsight, I really should have started to prepare for the switch at least a year before, and that's the advice I'd give anybody now who is in the same boat. The Auto-Cycle Union (ACU), which is the governing body of motorcycle sport in Great Britain, had recently started a course for young riders that specifically dealt with managing the transition between competing as a child and as an adult, but it was just a little bit late for me. I was supposed to attend one of the early classes, but after driving to Liverpool we discovered that the class had been cancelled and the ACU had forgotten to tell us. That went down well with my dad. Although they did cover his expenses.

Watching the adults as a spectator was a lot different to watching them as a competitor, and I went from thinking, *Wow, look at that, they're good*, to, *Shit, how on earth will I ever be able to do that?*

The one rider who really put this gap into perspective for me was the Spaniard Marc Colomer. He was the same age as me, so I compared myself to him. As a schoolboy he'd been as dominant in Spain as I'd been in Britain, but to be honest he was streets ahead of me. I remember seeing him in action once at the Scarborough International Youth Trial, which I'd ridden in a few times, and I was blown away by how good he was. Trials is a major sport in Spain, and the investment from sponsors and the manufacturers is massive, as are the crowds. Over here you might get a few hundred people attending an outdoor Trial, whereas over in Spain, especially for an indoor Trial, you'll get tens of thousands. They take the sport very seriously, and without wishing to denigrate our own efforts we just aren't in the same league as them. Or at least we weren't then. That investment was reflected in every aspect of Marc's performances, and the more I watched him ride the more despondent I became. He was the benchmark.

Fitness-wise, what I was lacking was strength. I was fit, but I wasn't naturally big or strong, and in the adult class you have to have both, but especially strength. That was something I should really have been working on in my teens, and when it finally dawned on me I could have kicked myself.

The sections in Trials aren't very long so although stamina's necessary it's not as important as strength. It's slightly different in events like the Scott Trial, and the Scottish Six Days Trial, as the distances you have to cover between sections are huge but generally it's strength that you have to worry about.

I actually went into that first year in the adult class with quite a lot of hope, as in addition to all the success I'd enjoyed as a child I'd just signed a three-year contract with Fantic. It was a dream come true, but instead of studying the contract beforehand, I just read the headlines, turned to the financial bit and signed it.

It was worth £2,000, which was a massive amount of money in the early 1990s. Or at least it was for a sixteen-year-old. I also thought that signing for a manufacturer, in whatever capacity, was as good as being a factory rider. It wasn't. Roy Carey was no longer the importer, more's the pity, and the man who'd taken over had, shall we say, different goals to those Roy and I had discussed. I wanted to progress and become world champion, and he wanted to get as many sponsor's stickers on the bike as soon as possible. This was understandable in a way, as he'd just taken over the business and wanted to sell bikes immediately, but with such conflicting ambitions, we were never going to see eye to eye, and as both of us became more and more frustrated the relationship deteriorated.

The first two rounds of the 1992 outdoor world championship took place in Spain and Belgium, but because I wasn't seventeen until April I wasn't old enough to drive to the events myself. If I'd had the guts, I'd have done so regardless, as I could already drive, but I was a good lad so stuck to the rules. In the end I made the trip with my mate David Pie. He wasn't really at the same level as me, but he wanted some experience at the worlds, so he drove, and we shared the costs.

As a schoolboy, if I ever rode abroad, Dad would always borrow a van from a man called David Jones, who rode for the Sittingbourne Trials Club and who ran a Mercedes dealership called Sparshatts. He was another one of my early benefactors, and shortly before I went professional he actually gave me my own van, an old Mercedes 609, and he even taxed and insured it for us. David's sadly no longer with us but if it hadn't been for him and Roy Carey and Roy Francis I wouldn't have been able to carry on competing as it would have become far too expensive.

Once we got the van back home, Dad immediately set about converting it into a cross between a workshop and a hotel in readiness for my travels and, as we hoped, world domination. Money was still very tight at the time, so it had to be done as cheaply as possible. He did a good job, though, and it was actually quite comfortable. That said, Dad could do nothing about the condensation that would gather on the inside of the roof. It was a bloody nightmare, as we'd often wake up soaking wet. The brakes were also a bit dodgy, and if you applied them going downhill, the entire van would shudder violently.

On the way to Belgium from Spain we had to drive through Andorra, and we got stuck in the snow. I remember me and David trying to put snow chains on the tyres and the stupid things kept coming off. We never made it over the mountain so did a three-hour detour. That was one of the few positives from that first year, the travelling. Every trip you make is an adventure, and despite freezing our balls off and having fights with snow chains it was better than being in an office.

Even at that age I'd already spent the vast majority of my life either riding or thinking about bikes and motorbikes, and I didn't know – or want – anything else. Maybe it was an omen that the only GCSE I passed was geography, and the only reason I was really interested in geography was because I wanted to win the world championship, and to win the world championship you had to travel – a lot! Some people get fed up with being on the road so much, but that's never affected me. For a start, it helps that I like to see new places, but a lot of the time you're travelling on your own, and that suits me down to the ground. In the early days it was all done in a van, like my old 609, and I must have driven tens of thousands of miles in it, once I'd passed my driving test!

These days I usually travel by plane. In fact, I must fly at least fifty or sixty times a year, perhaps more. I like being with other people, but I also like my own company and in that respect Trials and Hard Enduro have always suited me, as I get the best of both worlds. When I'm racing it's normally just me and the course, and that's where I'm happiest and most comfortable. There are spectators and other riders, of course, but most of the time they're there and gone in a flash. Then, when I've finished the race, I'll have a chat with some of the other riders or my mechanic and then go home to the family. I obviously love all that, but it's not long before I'm itching to get back on a bike again.

*

I ended up minding for David in Spain as I wasn't quite old enough to ride there, which was a bit of a new experience. A minder is somebody who assists a Trials rider during sections and will offer advice and physical help if they need it. Unfortunately, David ended up crashing out on every section, but

I enjoyed it while it lasted. The sections were absolutely enormous, and together with the crowds they seemed to represent perfectly Spain's dominance of the sport. Everything was just bigger! Again, this added to my anxieties about making it in the adult class, and I was glad that I wasn't riding there. Belgium was going to be my debut in the outdoor world championship, but if I thought it was going to be a lot easier than it was in Spain, I was mistaken. Yes, the sections were smaller and not quite as intimidating as they were in Spain, but they were tricky and very slippery. Over the two days of competition, I had all kinds of issues. I was, as I think I've already said, completely out of my depth. Or at least that's how it felt.

I ended up finishing thirty-first after only completing a couple of sections a lap. Had there been a hundred riders then thirty-first wouldn't have been too bad, but there were about sixty. I don't know what my scores were over the two days (and I don't want to know), but they must have been over a hundred, and I didn't score any championship points as it wasn't in the top fifteen.

To say that I left Belgium feeling disheartened would be a gigantic understatement. In addition to the result, I'd had all kinds of problems with the bike, and the importer, who was still my main point of contact, just wasn't interested. Also, travelling with a rider who didn't have much in the way of skill or experience meant there wasn't a lot of inspiration to be had on that first trip, least of all from my own performance.

When I got back home I sat down for a few days and tried to take stock. Whichever way I looked at it I just couldn't see how I'd be able to bridge the gap between me and the big boys, both in terms of ability and resources. The thing is, I was still the best young rider in the country at the time, with Dougie a very close second, but now that counted for absolutely nothing. Regardless of my age, I was now classed as an adult. That's what I couldn't get my head around. Progression and ambition are what had always driven me forward and I'd gone from having both to having none at all. Also, I wasn't the kind of person to go banging on people's doors and asking for help, so I had to learn to help myself.

Actually, I did manage to pluck up the courage to ask the factory teams for things like brake pads occasionally, and fortunately they almost always obliged with bits the factory riders had used. It wasn't easy, though. I used to sit there in the van and rehearse what I was going to say, as well as what I'd say if they told me to bugger off. They never did. I even used to get the odd tyre if I was really up against it. Seeing how the factory teams operated was a real eye-opener for me. The money being spent was astronomical, and I remember feeling impressed, jealous and slightly demoralised all at the same time. Who says men can't multi-task?

I ended up riding a further six rounds at the 1992 outdoor world championship: the British round was held in Fort William; in France, it was at Eymoutiers; in Andorra, at La Rabassa; then Nepomuk, Czech Republic; Stryszów, Poland; and at Camerino in Italy. My best result was seventeenth in Poland where I did OK because it was a muddy Trial. I still didn't score any championship points, though, as they were awarded only for the first fifteen places, so it was hardly a success. There was no progress, as such. I was just relying on what I was good at.

The man who minded for me at the majority of these Trials

was a mate of mine called Jon Martin. Because Jon had a job, he'd fly out at the last minute, so I'd drive to the Trials on my own which meant I had to hone my map-reading skills very quickly. This was one of the few upsides to my debut year and is probably what kept me going. Well, that and a bit of fortitude. Being quiet is seen as a weakness by some, but I'd have to disagree. I'd been independent from a very early age and that had come from keeping my head down and just getting on with things. What's that old saying? *Never underestimate the determination of a quiet man.* Well, I wasn't quite a man yet – not in the legal sense, as I wasn't yet eighteen – but I was determined. I had to be.

The round in Germany was a little bit different as I had my brother minding me. Despite the age difference we'd always been quite close, Barry and I, and because he'd ridden Trials before I thought yes, why not. Unfortunately, this closeness was tested on the third section. I was trying to scale a step when I started to struggle and instead of catching me or the bike he missed and the bike went flying. My result from the round immediately prior to this had been twentieth and although that was an improvement on the overall result from the first round I was still pointless. And I was angry.

'Why the bloody hell didn't you catch me?' I shouted at my brother. 'Look at the bloody bike!'

He didn't have to say anything. The look he gave me said it all!

'You were the one who messed up,' he eventually said.

'Yes, and you were supposed to catch me!'

My brother and I always used to argue as kids – what brothers don't – but we'd never had an argument in a situation like that before. Although we made it up again later that was the first and last time my brother minded for me, and just to set the record straight, it *was* my fault. There, I've said it, and it's only taken me twenty years!

4

The first decision I made after completing my debut year as an adult was to change bikes. Or at least get rid of the one I had. The relationship between me and the Fantic importer had deteriorated to such an extent that we were hardly even talking, and that was no use to anyone. I didn't need to be a factory rider – although I would have liked to have been – but what I did need was a good working relationship with both the importer and, if possible, the manufacturer of whatever bike I was riding, so with neither of those things in place I had no choice other than to break the contract. Another reason for me wanting out was that I hadn't read the financial part of the contract properly and instead of me getting £2,000 a year it was £2,000 for three years!

In the end I had to pay two-thirds of my money back, which wasn't ideal, as that accounted for virtually every penny I'd managed to save up. Also, despite being a free agent I was now without a ride for the coming season and this quickly became a massive worry for me. Something had to change, and it had to change quickly.

Fortunately, shortly after leaving Fantic I was approached

by another Trials legend, Malcolm Rathmell. He'd heard I'd been having problems and claimed to have a solution.

Like Mick Andrews, Malcolm Rathmell's reputation goes before him and together with Mick, Yrjö Vesterinen and his best friend Martin Lampkin, he all but dominated the sport throughout the 1970s. I had already met Malcolm once or twice, briefly, but this was the first time I'd had a conversation with him.

'Eh up youngen, I hear you might be looking for a new bike,' said Malcolm.

'That's right,' I replied. 'I am.'

'How about I send you a bike to have a look at?'

In 1991 Malcolm had started importing Aprilia motorbikes from Italy, and he'd since worked with the likes of Steve Saunders and Stefan Merriman. Fortunately for me he was looking for a second rider for 1993, and he asked me if I'd be interested in having a look at an Aprilia. The bike wasn't the best but getting involved with somebody of that magnitude and with so many contacts was exactly what I needed, and it couldn't have come at a better time.

According to Malcolm, one of the first things that had brought me to his attention, apart from riding, was my vocabulary. Malcolm thinks it happened in Germany, but after having a really bad round one day he overheard me giving myself a bollocking and decided to stop and listen. Apparently I was sitting on my own, and I was using some fairly colourful language. This is just a vague memory to me, but Malcolm remembers it well. What struck him the most was how angry I was, and he walked away impressed. I don't remember this, but Malcolm says we had a quick chat later that day, although he can't remember what about. Knowing him he probably offered me a few words of advice and commiseration. Or called me a daft bugger!

A few days after speaking to Malcolm, a shiny new Aprilia turned up at my house and after pulling it out of its box I kicked it over. For some reason it immediately started revving flat out and after a minute or two it seized up. I'd only had it a few minutes! The only thing I could do was call Malcolm and when I told him what had happened there was a long pause. 'I'll send somebody down,' he said eventually. I think the only thing that stopped him from giving me a mouthful was that he was keen on signing me, but I have a fairly good idea what he'd have said once he put the phone down.

Malcolm ended up sending a mechanic down called Colin Boniface and according to him the reason it revved up was because the throttle had stuck open in the box. Lesson number one from Mr Rathmell; always make sure the throttle flicks back!

After eventually signing with Malcolm, who was based in North Yorkshire, I decided to move up there myself. Actually, that's not strictly true. What happened was I went to Yorkshire to practise for what was meant to be a few days and just never came back. I had asked Mum and Dad if we could move there, but they always said no.

'But they've got rocks up there,' I used to plead.

'That's not a good enough reason for us to move the entire family two hundred and fifty miles north, Graham!'

'Fair enough.'

Yorkshire was, and still is, the capital of Trials and if I wanted to progress and be at the heart of the sport it was where I had to be. That's why I never left it. Well, that and the rocks. I was obsessed.

The people I initially stayed with were the Hemingway family in East Keswick which is near Leeds. After Lampkin, Hemingway is one of the most familiar surnames on the British Trials scene, with Dan, Ben and their father John all competing to a very high standard. Dan and Ben, who are both a bit younger than me, also ride Hard Enduro, so I see them quite a lot these days.

I had about a week with the Hemingways, and they were very hospitable. Unfortunately, I had an accident during one of the practice sessions and ended up hurting my elbow. The next morning, when I woke up, there was blood all over the bed. I was mortified! That was the first bad accident I'd had since riding as an adult and it took me about an hour to pluck up the courage to tell Mrs Hemingway what had happened. 'Excuse me, Mrs Hemingway,' I said. 'I'm afraid I've made a mess of my bed.' God only knows what she thought. She was very nice about it, though.

After that I went to practise with Robert Crawford and the aforementioned Colin Boniface, who, as well as working for Malcolm, was also Robert's mechanic. Robert, who is from Northern Ireland, is about three years older than me and in 1990 he'd shocked the Trials world by finishing seventh in the outdoor world championship riding a Beta. The year before that, aged just seventeen, he'd won the Irish championship, and he too had been touted as a future world champion. After finishing seventh in 1990, Robert had been signed by Montesa who were easily the richest and most powerful team (they still are), but in the two years he'd ridden for them he struggled to build on that initial promise and had finished twelfth in 1991 and fifteenth in 1992. In 1993 he'd signed with Malcolm so basically we were team mates.

Colin and Robert had rented a house together at the bottom of Pendle Hill, which is in the wilds of east Lancashire, so that's where I initially stayed. Unfortunately they weren't getting on at the time, and when I arrived the atmosphere was pretty awful. Even so, I'd much rather be living with a Trials star and his mechanic while at loggerheads and surrounded by rocks than I would in Kent surrounded by mud. At the end of the day I was there to practise and try and further my career, so they could argue all they liked. When I first arrived I was obviously a welcome distraction for Robert and Colin. I learnt so much and although it was a tense environment, I really appreciate my time with them now.

This house they'd rented had no hot water or heating and was like something out of a different century. That said, I enjoyed chopping logs for the fire in the snow. It was also miles away from anywhere, so with Robert and Colin arguing and the house being pretty bleak I spent almost every waking hour practising. It was brilliant!

At the beginning of 1993 we moved from Bleak House, as I used to call it, to a place called Silsden, near Skipton in North Yorkshire. Those of you who are Trials enthusiasts will know exactly why Silsden is significant to the sport, but for those who aren't, allow me to enlighten you.

Silsden is, for want of a better phrase, Lampkin country, and at the time the entire family lived there. There was Arthur Lampkin, who, to the older generations is probably better known than Dougie; his brother Sid, who'd won the Scottish Six Days Trial and the Scott Trial and who'd been a BSA factory rider alongside Arthur in the 1960s; Martin – or Mart, as he was known – who was Dougie's father and who'd won the inaugural outdoor world championship in 1975, not to mention the Scottish Six Days Trial and the Scott Trial; John, who is Arthur's son and who'd been a regular top-ten competitor throughout the 1980s in the outdoor world championship and who had become the UK importer for Beta; and of course, Dougie, who'd recently made the transition from schoolboy to adult and who was about to make his debut in the world championship.

At the time, Dougie's mum and dad owned the newsagents in Silsden and if Mart was ever serving when I went in to buy something I'd get really nervous. He was one of the friendliest people you could ever meet and would talk to anybody. I was always a bit star-struck, though, and would just smile and walk out. I remember thinking to myself once, *How cool is this? I just bought a Mars Bar from a world champion!* It was great having somebody like that on your doorstep.

I forgot to mention that Steve Colley was also living in Silsden at the time. Although we didn't get on that well, he was having a lot of success and was another reason why it was good to be there. It was like the Trials version of Monaco really!

One of the other reasons we decided to move to Silsden, apart from the house near Pendle Hill being bleak, cold and even a bit creepy at times, was Addingham Moorside. When it comes to Trials, Addingham Moorside is God's own practice area and it's where Dougie and his family – not to mention hundreds of other riders – had all honed their craft. Being able to practise on Addingham Moorside day in day out was a dream come true for me, and because Silsden was such a significant area for the sport, I felt in a way like I'd arrived. I was still the poor relation, but with Rob, Colin, Steve and the Lampkins on my doorstep I was where I needed to be. Geographically, at least.

The only reason I'd been able to pay for all this – the rent and running a bike, etc. – was because I'd taken some part-time jobs before travelling up. I had a paper round for a while, did some apple picking, and I also worked in a postal sorting office – anything just to keep my head above water. I actually enjoyed working and especially the apple picking, as the more you picked the more you got paid, and I was the fastest – obviously. I didn't mind the paper round, as I used to fly round on my BMX. It was like an Enduro with deliveries. I also did a couple of weeks with my dad building a car wash at an Esso garage, which was interesting. I was useless, though. Believe it or not, given the kind of terrain I ride over, I'm quite scared of heights, and I ended up just fetching and carrying. I know people often claim that they're born to do what they do, but I genuinely cannot do anything other than ride a bike. I've got no qualifications (apart from the GCSE in geography) and was always too busy riding to even think about getting a trade. According to my girlfriend Sandra I'm quite a good cook, but apart from that, I'm useless!

One thing I started doing more of when I moved up north, as well as practising on rocks, was going to the gym. Rob had taken me to one while we were living at Bleak House, but unfortunately I didn't pass the induction, so I was barred. It was quite professional, this place, and when we arrived the instructor, who was massive and quite scary looking, took one look at me and asked me if I knew what I was doing.

'Of course I do,' I lied. 'I've been to the gym loads of times back home.'

'Oh aye?' said the instructor suspiciously. 'You see that

machine over there? Go and show me how it works.'

This was obviously health and safety 1990s style!

The machine in question was a bench-presser and although I know that now I didn't then. Subsequently, I made a complete arse of myself trying to operate the machine and after trying a few times the instructor, who I don't think liked southerners, called me something like a big southern jessie and asked me to leave. It was a proper dollop of northern hospitality!

I ended up going to a place called Bill's Gym, which was, shall we say, a little bit old-school. There were no machines and because there were no machines there was no induction. It was also cheap, which was good, so with plenty of free weights knocking around and no instructors I was able to concentrate on building up my strength. That had actually been going quite well since moving up north and I'd put on at least a stone. I probably wasn't eating the right diet at the time but that was down to money more than anything else as every penny I had went on getting me to the rounds so I just ate pasta and tinned tomatoes. That really was it for me. It was hardly balanced, and I was getting next to no protein. Oh well, I'd learn. One day.

One of my ambitions for 1993 was to try and find a regular minder and preferably one who could double up as a mechanic. In the end I managed to find a lad called Paul Dixon, and I paid him on a race-by-race basis, although not very much. He also shared the driving and was in charge of the music, which consisted of one cassette featuring some really bad music from the '80s. The radio didn't work very well so if we ever wanted music, that was it. It was played over and over and halfway through a round one of the songs would pop into my head and stay there for the rest of the day. It was torture.

In the back of the van we had a cooker on which I'd prepare my pasta and chopped tomatoes. Nine times out of ten I'd balance my plate on the steering wheel to eat (while stationary, of course) but more often than not half of it would end up on the floor. This was never a problem, as we had an ant's nest underneath the passenger seat and within minutes of us dropping any food on the floor they would march out, pick it up and take it to the nest. You probably think I'm joking about this, but I'm not. It's safe to say I'm not the cleanest person in the world, so it was actually a really good arrangement. I dropped food a lot and the ants cleared it up. Somebody once complained that it was unhygienic to have an ant's nest in a van, so I put down some jam thinking that they'd come along and get stuck in it. Wrong! I came back about an hour later and it had all gone. After receiving another complaint I again tried to get rid of the nest, but by that time they'd moved down to the chassis. I just let them get on with it. They must have been some of the most widely travelled and best fed ants in the world. I remember John Lampkin coming up to me once and saying that somebody had broken into my van. 'They've made a right mess of it,' he said. 'You'd better go and have a look.' After running over I had a look through the driver's window and from what I could remember it was exactly as I'd left it. I became quite famous for having a messy van; to be honest, nothing's really changed.

As well as a cooker we also had a small sink in the van which would empty into a bucket that we placed underneath. I have an absolutely shocking memory when it comes to things like this and it didn't matter how many times I told myself to check underneath the van, I'd always just drive off and one year I actually drove over the bucket! Years later, when I was riding in my first Erzberg, this ended in disaster. Well, maybe not a disaster but it was a bit of an inconvenience. Some people had left some bags of rubbish by my van and because I didn't check underneath I ended up driving over them. Unfortunately, there was a bloody tent pole among this rubbish and it ended up going right through my fuel tank. All I could do was leave the pole in, and drive home for seventeen hours with diesel dripping out of the side.

Dougie Lampkin ended up travelling with us for much of 1993 – for the world rounds, at least – and it was a massive learning experience. Although Dougie had his whole family behind him, I think they wanted him to experience the real world of low-budget competing. He was also extraordinarily talented, of course, but I don't think anyone had any idea how successful he'd become. I did appreciate, however, that all the support Dougie received brought with it an awful lot of pressure, and that was something I'd experienced myself to a certain extent from being referred to as 'the next big thing'. Being the talented son of the inaugural outdoor world champion meant that you were expected to follow in his foot-steps, so Dougie had a hell of a lot to live up to. He seemed to handle it very well though and I think I probably found the situation a lot more difficult than he did. Dougie also jelled a lot more with Paul Dixon as they were both northern monkeys and I was a shandy-drinking southerner, so I ended up on my own a lot of the time. It was my own fault really, and in hindsight I could probably have tried a bit harder to get involved in the conversations. I was still struggling for results though and had started getting more stressed around events. Subsequently, I tended to avoid talking to anyone, and with Dougie performing well the last person I wanted to see at the end of a round was him.

Because Dougie wasn't old enough to drive, Paul and I used to do it, and the only time the three of us ever argued was when we had to use a map. I dread to think how many arguments or divorces have been caused by maps over the years, but if sat nav hadn't been invented there'd have been a hell of a lot more. I remember we got lost one day and after driving here, there and everywhere for about half an hour Paul, who was the one holding the map, asked me if I had any idea where we were. 'You're the one with the fucking map,' I snapped. 'Here,' he said, 'you have a go,' and then threw the map at me. Unfortunately the window was open and it flew straight out and ended up in a large puddle in the middle of the road. Did I mention it had been raining for some time?

As soon as it was safe to do so I pulled over into a lay-by and the three of us just looked at each other. After a few seconds we all started laughing but that soon stopped when we remembered about the map and ran back to fish it out of the puddle. A few pages were unreadable and the Northerners were too tight to buy a new one, so we struggled on.

Despite my nerves often getting the better of me, my main issue with regards to my results in 1993 was the bike. Tommi Ahvala had won the previous year's outdoor world championship on an Aprilia, so I was naturally quite excited and optimistic about riding for them. Unfortunately, the bike they gave me had a Rotax engine which was heavy and out of date compared to other brands. It also had an angled shock which was nowhere near as developed as the tighter upright shocks on other bikes. It felt heavy and more like an Enduro bike. Subsequently, I finished the first round of the 1993 outdoor world championship in twenty-fifth place – two places below the position I'd finished in the last round of 1992. The next three rounds, which were in Belgium, Germany and the Czech Republic, yielded similar results. Despite me having signed with Malcolm and the current world championship-winning manufacturer, I was still a world away from making any kind of impact.

5

In between competing in the outdoor world championship and the European championship, which I'll come on to, I managed to find the time, and the money, to travel to Spain for a bit of practice. It was just me and the van this time, so I only had to find the money for petrol and pasta. And tinned tomatoes. I was due to practise with Tommi Awhala and I remember sleeping outside the house and waiting for him to get up. He got the shock of his life when he saw me!

In 1993 the FIM started the European Trials championship, which is basically a feeder competition for up-and-coming talent. This competition was a bit of a godsend for me, as it allowed me to go back a step and compete with riders who were the same age and who were either at a similar level or just below. It allowed me to regain a little bit of confidence as I was finishing in the top five and without wanting to sound melodramatic it might well have saved my career.

At the German round, which took place in Thalheim in the former East Germany, something very sad but quite extraordinary happened. A few weeks before, a friend and competitor of mine called David Page had died of leukaemia.

Born in Scotland, David had won the 1992 Scottish Trials Championship and together with the likes of Dougie, Steve Colley and me was talked about as being one of the next big things. We went back a long way, David and me, and as well as being a very natural and talented rider he always had a smile on his face. He obviously loved what he did and he was liked by everyone.

While on a trip to Italy with his father Ernie to watch the Italian round of the world championship, David had started to feel ill and was rushed home to Edinburgh. Just days later he was diagnosed as having leukaemia and tragically died only a few weeks later. His death had naturally shocked the world of Trials, and Ernie, who had always been a regular on the scene and was naturally David's biggest fan, just disappeared.

Then, about a week before the German round of the European championship I got a call from him. He was travelling to the round with Dougie and Mart Lampkin in his motor-home and wanted to know if I needed a lift and a minder. 'Yes please,' was my immediate answer, so the following week we all set off to Thalheim. Mart and Ernie were friends from way back, which meant the banter was continuous. David's death must still have been very raw for Ernie, but the fact that he was attending a Trial again was good news, especially as he was with Mart. The only thing that worried me slightly was how Ernie might react when minding for somebody other than David. It was obviously going to be emotional no matter what, and I'd be lying if I said that the idea hadn't made me feel slightly uncomfortable. At least at first.

As you might expect, the majority of the conversations tended to emanate from Martin and Ernie's mouths – as always, I was far happier listening than talking. From a Trials rider's point of view, and especially one who is on their way to a competition, when somebody like Martin Lampkin talks, you listen (in Mart's case you had very little choice!) and I was like a sponge in that respect. All the way there, Mart and Ernie trotted out story after story after story, and every so often a bit of advice would be thrown back to Dougie and me. Just like Ernie and David, Martin and Dougie were very close, and because they understood each other so well Dougie was able to benefit fully from his dad's experience. I haven't witnessed many relationships like that before, in any sport. It was unique.

My two results prior to this round in the European championship had been fourth and fifth, and with my confidence growing a bit I'd been daring to dream about finishing on the podium. I wasn't sure at what event, and frankly I didn't care, but I was hoping it would either be here or at the next round.

Because of Ernie, the emotions I experienced prior to the start were different to what they usually were, and instead of it being all about me and what was going to happen in the Trial, the majority of my thoughts were about David and Ernie. In a way that seemed to take the pressure off, and although I felt emotional I was far less nervous. Ernie, on the other hand, was emotional right from the start, but he held it together brilliantly and was a fantastic minder. I could tell, though, that every piece of advice and every word of encouragement was in honour of David, and I wanted to win it for both of them. I wish I could remember more about the Trial itself, but I have to admit it's all a bit of a blur. I suppose I was in the zone.

When I found out that I'd won the round, Ernie started to cry, and later on when no one was looking, so did I. Looking back that was easily the most emotional experience of my life so far, but it was also the most gratifying. Just a year earlier I'd been in turmoil, and everything was pointing to me either continuing to deteriorate or dropping out of Trials altogether. That's not being defeatist. I just couldn't see where a win was going to come from, let alone a bike or a sponsor. Then all of a sudden the telephone rings and before I know it I'm listening to Ernie and Mart Lampkin on a road trip to Germany and then I'm standing on a podium – right in the middle. Although the circumstances were very sad, my first win in an international Trials competition was extremely special, and I have Ernie to thank for that. And David.

I finished the 1993 European championship in fifth position, and the three riders on the podium were Dougie, Cesar Panicot and Dario Re Delle Gandine. Was I pissed off that Dougie had overtaken me in his first year as an adult? Of course I was. I'm only human. There was nothing I could do about it, though, and I had to try and concentrate on the progress I'd made, as opposed to the progress that Dougie had made. He was bloody good, though. There's no getting away from it.

During the Spanish round of the European championship there was a downhill section that nobody had been able to negotiate. Everybody had put a foot down, including me, but when Dougie rolled up you got a feeling that things might change. Mart, who was minding for Dougie, had been uncharacteristically quiet up until then, and when Dougie rolled off the top of this section and cleared it Mart just exploded. I remember hearing him shout in his broad Yorkshire accent,

'BEAUUUUTIFUL, DOUGIE! BEAUUUUUUTIFUL!'
He was like a foghorn.

Looking back, it was actually quite a privilege watching Dougie make the transition from schoolboy to adult, and as time went on he obviously just got better and better. He's the best Trials rider we've ever had in my opinion.

I think what I lacked in those early days – and throughout the majority of my Trials career – was confidence. I certainly had the potential. There's no question about that. There were no sports psychologists at the very start of my professional career. It was just me, myself and I. I'd been able to make my own decisions, but not all of those decisions had been good ones, and I was always a bit short on advice. Being quiet and, in some people's eyes, standoffish, meant that this was rarely forthcoming, so I suppose you could say I was flawed in that respect, which diminished my chances of success. It wasn't all doom and gloom, however, and I took heart from the fact that I'd got this far almost single-handedly.

I also managed to score my first points in a world championship in 1993, which meant that by the end of the year my championship tally in both the worlds and Europeans was two points in the worlds and a win in the Europeans. Those two points meant that I finished twenty-second in the worlds which, given my age and situation with regards to things like cash and equipment, was bordering on being respectable. I managed to win those two points in Poland, and because of the field – Dougie, Marc Colomer and Jordi Tarrés, etc. – they meant almost as much as the win in Germany. The Trial itself was quite a muddy one which was similar to the south east of England so I felt quite at home. That said, I was still miles away on things like rock steps and the bigger sections as they weren't my forte and I hadn't had much practice. It was a start, though.

Something else I struggled with that year was the heat, and I almost fainted in France. Two laps in and I had no energy left, but rather than going back to the van and trying to rehydrate myself after finishing the lap, I sat down and opened a tin of rice pudding. That was always my treat after an event, and for some reason at that moment I preferred it to water! After finishing the rice pudding I felt no better and after puking my guts up I started falling about all over the place. Water would have been better!

The only protein I ever really ate at that time was tinned meat, which was obviously just processed rubbish. I used to go to Farm Foods before a trip and buy about ten tins of tinned tomatoes, five tins of rice pudding, two or three tins of beef stew and a big bag of pasta twirls. If only we'd had strength and conditioning coaches or YouTube back then. I needed taking in hand.

What the heat also did, apart from giving me a craving for rice pudding, was highlight my lack of fitness. I don't remember seeing any of the other riders suffering as much as me, so although I had some stamina I just didn't have enough strength and power.

In the world championship I was struggling competitively, but in the Europeans I was always in contention. That feeling of making progress again was a huge boost for me. Before the win in Germany and the points in Poland, I was beginning to feel like it had been forever since I'd enjoyed any success. No wonder I was beginning to doubt myself.

The most important lesson I learned that year, apart from learning how to win again, was how to manage my own expectations. With nobody guiding my career and my nerves often getting the better of me, that was essential. The only way I could continue without going bonkers was to take it one race at a time, and ambitions of winning world championships and the like would have to be quelled. At least for now.

What I really needed at this point in my career – and my life in general – was a mentor. Somebody who could help me with every aspect of my game and, as I just said, take me in hand.

As it turned out, I was in luck.

At the end of 1993 my Aprilia deal had come to an end and Malcolm had stopped importing them. I don't know the full ins and outs, but I think they'd stopped manufacturing Trials bikes, so it was just one of those things. Then, at the start of 1994, Bruno Camozi at Scorpa started touting a new Trials prototype. I'd started getting invited to some indoor Trials out in France and while attending one with Rob Crawford, I saw the Scorpa people talking to some riders about this prototype of his. It turned out they were also looking for an importer in the UK, and to cut a long story short they found Malcolm. Or Malcolm found them.

On a trip to the new Scorpa factory in France soon after this, Malcolm's son Martin and I drove out. Martin runs the business with Malcolm and Rhoda. He can be quite impatient, can Martin, and after falling asleep in the passenger seat one afternoon while he was driving, I woke up to find we were tearing along the hard shoulder doing a crazy overtaking manoeuvre to save time. It was a memorable experience though and some important time spent at the factory.

The good news was I had a bike for 1994. The bad news was it was shit. Just like the Aprilia it had a Rotax engine and was very heavy. In fact, it was built like a tank but the positive was that I could practise all day every day without much maintenance. At the end of the day it was a prototype, so we just had to hope they kept working on it.

At the risk of sounding like a whinging old git, it obviously makes a difference what kind of bike you have, and the difference then between the bikes that were being ridden by the top three or four riders and the rest of the field was vast. The reason these boys had the best bikes was because they were the best riders, so at the end of the day the only way to catch up was to knuckle down and work harder than anyone else.

Fortunately, there are still plenty of events in the Trials calendar where privateers can compete at the highest level and go up against the best, such as at the Scott Trial and the Scottish Six Days Trial, and that, in my opinion, is the beauty of Trials. The sport I'm currently involved in, Hard Enduro, is like Trials was thirty years ago in that you have a few professionals and loads of privateers, but at least we've got that model to follow. Having everybody lumped in together is great, but it's good to have an elite event sitting at the top of the sport. You know, the best versus the best.

To be fair, and in an attempt to sound a bit more positive for a change, the Aprilia had actually been quite a good bike to learn on. For a start it was sturdy and because you didn't have to change the clutch plates you could just hammer it every day, which I did! In that respect it was one of the best bikes I ever had, and it would hold up to just about anything. It was rubbish for hopping and bopping, though, which was pretty essential. That was the worst thing.

The Scorpa prototype was quite similar to the Aprilia and must have been at least three or four kilos heavier than the majority of bikes. Again, I'm not trying to make excuses here, as at the end of the day I had a bike and was grateful. It was just big and clumsy.

The most positive thing to happen to me at the start of 1994 was getting a bigger commitment from Malcolm and his wife Rhoda, which is what I alluded to earlier. The arrangement with Rob Crawford hadn't worked out for them, and I was going to need as much help as I could get. In the end, with a bit of persuasion from me, they suggested that I go and live with them. So, not only would I be riding for Malcolm, but I'd be living under his and Rhoda's roof. It was a full commitment from both sides and was just what I needed.

The day I went to live there, Rhoda took me to one side and said, 'If you give Malcolm and me one hundred per cent, we'll always do the same for you.' All three of us were true to our word throughout the relationship, and I could not have felt more loyal to Malcolm and Rhoda, nor they to me.

It really was the opportunity I needed. Malcolm become my minder and mentor, and with Rhoda looking after the domestic side of things I was able to concentrate all my efforts on working with Malcolm, honing my skills and, hopefully, winning a few Trials.

I have to say that Malcolm and Rhoda were both very welcoming, and they didn't seem to mind me being shy. Rhoda's also a brilliant cook, so as well as having something different to pasta and tinned tomatoes, which must have been a massive shock to my system, I was actually eating protein that wasn't out of a tin.

Looking back, I was very fortunate to have been given this opportunity and I'll always be very grateful to them. I don't know if it was out of sympathy or because of my potential but they must have thought I deserved a chance at least. I'm very glad they did. If they hadn't, God knows what would have happened. Probably very little with regards to progress.

As with Mart Lampkin, when somebody like Malcolm Rathmell talks you listen, and although Malcolm didn't talk nearly as often or as loudly as his old friend and competitor, whenever he did attempt to impart some information or advice it was always sound – and it was always appreciated. He was a hard task master, though, and he didn't take any crap. If Malcolm thought you weren't pulling your weight or you weren't concentrating he'd tell you, and he'd do the same if you made a mistake. He was old-school.

A little while ago I asked Malcolm what I was like when I first came to live with him and Rhoda, and his exact words were, 'You wanted to know the far end of a fart and which way the stink went.' Translated, this apparently means I was very inquisitive and wanted to learn as much as I could.

A few months after I moved in, Malcolm was asked by a friend of his why he was putting so much time and effort into me.

'I keep giving him stick and he keeps coming back for more,' was Malcolm's terse response. That just about sums it up.

One of my biggest problems when I went to Malcolm's was my lack of mechanical knowledge. I'm going to try and write this how he said it: 'You were crap and you didn't know't back wheel from't front.' It was a fair point and I remember him then saying to me that from now on, every time I went out on my bike I had to 'fettle' it afterwards. This was a new word to me and basically means 'to maintain' in Yorkshire. Since going to live at Malcolm and Rhoda's I'd been throwing in a few *'eh ups'* just to try and fit in. Rhoda's a fellow southerner so whenever I got stuck she would always translate. Within a few months I'd found my way around my bike and I was actually interested in how it worked – and how I could keep it working. I would wash it off after nearly every practice session, cleaning the carb and filter, and would spend three to four days 'fettling it' before a British event. It was like learning a new language, I suppose, and the more I learned the more I wanted to know.

One night before a race I stripped a thread in the cylinder and went looking for Malcolm. 'Will it take long?' I asked him. 'No, don't worry,' he said. 'It'll only take five minutes.' But when Malcolm had a look I'd knackered it. We had to drill it out and put a helicoil in. We didn't finish until about two o'clock in the morning. He only showed me once, by the way!

I suppose the only slight downside to my new arrangement was that I wasn't earning much money. Then again, I didn't need very much. I'd lost a bit of independence, I suppose, but it was a small price to pay. In fact, I'd probably earned no more than about £2,000 in 1993, which I'd won competing in smaller events, but if I could ride my bike and wasn't losing money, I was happy.

Malcolm and Rhoda's final investment in team Jarvis prior to the 1994 season, on top of all the chicken I was scoffing, was a caravan that we towed with my van. Malcolm and Rhoda slept in the caravan, and I slept in the van with the ants. For the first time ever I could see the floor in the back of the van as Malcolm had ordered me to clear all the crap out so he could fill it with spare parts. Getting the caravan was essential really as even if it had just been Malcolm and me, he'd never have put up with sleeping in an ant-infested van. Not with all my mess.

Incidentally, Malcolm used to call my van a *Rolls Canardly*, as in it rolled downhill but could hardly get up again. Its other name was Big Bertha, which I think Rhoda coined; both names suited it perfectly. Its top speed was about 65mph flat-out, so you can imagine how long it took to get to somewhere like Poland! Although when I travelled with Dougie and Paul we would get 72mph downhill in neutral. 'Knock it out of cog,' Doug would say. It saved fuel and the environment, of course.

Regarding spare parts, the rule was that whenever I used something I had to write it down on a pad which was hung up in the back so it could be replaced. Again, this was alien to me, but it was crucial to running a team, and especially a small team like ours. It took me a while to come around, and I remember receiving one or two bollockings before it finally hit home.

'If you use a throttle cable, Graham, bloody well replace it!'

Life on the road with Malcolm and Rhoda was pretty idyllic really, and the majority of my memories are good ones. As far as the Trials were concerned, we had a pretty professional set-up, and because Rhoda looked after us so well I was again able to concentrate on riding. We did have one or two mishaps, though. I remember the A-frame on the caravan snapped in Poland one year. I learned a lot of new Yorkshire words that day, courtesy of my mentor. To be fair

I think it frightened Malcolm to death. It certainly did me. One minute were doing about 40mph then suddenly, bang! Malcolm had some insurance sponsorship with the RAC at the time, but instead of writing it off they towed it all the way back to Britain. Malcolm was gutted! The problem was that Big Bertha was quite a sturdy vehicle and she shook the caravan to bits. It was an ongoing issue.

The only problem with having a mentor – again, this was down to me – is that whenever I rode badly I'd often feel like I'd let Malcolm down and would beat myself up about it for hours or even days afterwards. As I said earlier, Malcolm was old-school, so there'd be no arm around the shoulder if I did badly. That was Rhoda's job. It must have been frustrating for him when progress was slow and the results weren't coming, but at the end of the day Malcolm just wanted me to win, and I'm sure that when he'd failed in his early days there were no pats on the back or shouts of 'Better luck next time, Malcolm.' He was simply using his knowledge and experience (and his vocabulary, which was interesting) to try and turn me into the best rider I could possibly be, and I'm the first to admit that I must have been quite a frustrating pupil at times. If Malcolm reads this book, which he might, if I give him a free copy, I'm sure he'll be nodding when he gets to this bit. I think he was expecting some kind of reaction when he gave me a bollocking – something like, 'Right, I'm going to prove you wrong, Malcolm!' – but he never got one. Not verbally, at least. I'd just stand there, say nothing and go a bit red. I'd always take his advice on board, though, and would always endeavour to come back a better rider. At the end of the day, that was the reaction Malcolm really wanted. With us two, actions always spoke louder than words.

I remember one time at a world round there was a nasty downhill with some loose rocks and just before the bottom I lost the front end and went flying. While I was trying to pick myself up, Malcolm looked at me and said, 'What the fuck are you doing?' and before I could answer he walked off in disgust. The reason he got angry is because I wasn't paying attention and Malcolm knew that. I told you I was frustrating.

The biggest bollocking Malcolm ever gave me happened at the Scottish Six Days Trial, but I have no idea when, as I've been trying to block it out! I certainly deserved it though, as it was a monumental cock-up.

I was sitting outside a checkpoint after returning to parc fermé when all of a sudden Malcolm, Rhoda and my dad turned up in the van.

'What the bloody hell are you doing sat there?' asked Malcolm.

'Waiting for you,' I replied.

'You have handed your timecard in, haven't you?' he said, more in hope than expectation.

I remember thinking, *oh shit!*

I ran to the checkpoint, but I was already two minutes too late. Malcolm just exploded! In fact, I think everybody did apart from me. I felt like such a tit. Sometimes I was in a world of my own.

In truth, I probably needed to toughen up a bit, so if Malcolm had treated me with kid gloves when I was with him, it would have done me a lot more harm than good. Before being taken on by him I just wasn't fit enough, either physically or mentally, and Malcolm probably knew that better than I did. I've never actually sat down and discussed this with

Malcolm, but I'm pretty sure that everything he did was for a reason, and the effects of his and Rhoda's care and influence were both immediate and far reaching.

With the world championship not starting until the middle of April my first round with Malcolm and Rhoda and the new Scorpa was going to be in Spain on 20th March in the first round of the 1994 European championship. The bike was still heavy, but my fitness had improved massively, as had my diet. That was down to Rhoda, of course, who had become like a surrogate mother to me. Because of her care the only stresses I had, apart from the bike, were of my own making, and it was up to me to sort them out. My mental strength was improving almost by the day and having a living legend with me at every event did me a power of good. How could it not? Trials may have progressed since his day with different techniques, bikes and tyres, etc., but the fundamentals are the same, as is the desire to win. That will never change.

Dougie, having won the European championship the previous year, had moved up to the worlds but with him were a bunch of young Spaniards who were all hungry for glory. There seemed to be an endless stream of talent coming out of Spain at that time and the overall standard was incredibly high. The sections at the European championship that year had been on the easy side, but with the dry dusty conditions I was happy to come away with third.

At the following round, which was in France, I finished first. I could be wrong, but I'm pretty sure Malcolm cracked a smile when that happened, although he might have just banged his foot. I then went on to win again in Norway, which was brilliant, and after finishing every other race on the podium I went into the final round in first place. Although I didn't consider it to be a formality, I was confident that the final round was going to be win number three and see me crowned the overall winner. The rider in second place was only a couple of points behind me, though, so I knew I'd have to perform. I was confident. Confident in myself, confident in Malcolm, and even confident in my bike. Or at least more confident.

Incidentally, the world championship, which had started in April, had again demonstrated the gulf between the top five in the sport and everyone else, as they were just streets ahead, although from my own point of view the difference was now a bit less pronounced. At the first round, which was at Kilbroney Park in Ireland, I'd finished thirteenth, so at least I'd scored points straight away. That had been a massive boost to me as it had made me feel like I was competing as opposed to just taking part and by the time we got to round seven, which was in Italy, I'd finished in the points on no fewer than four occasions, with my best result being twelfth. Better still, I'd secured that result at the Great Britain round in Houghton Park, and from then on my sole ambition for 1994, apart from becoming the European champion, of course, was to finish in the top ten at a world championship round for the first time. Unfortunately, it wasn't to be, as I broke my thumb at round eight of the championship, in Biasca in Switzerland. It was just one of those things. I hit a step, my back wheel slipped off, and the next thing I remember I was sitting there clutching my thumb and reciting some of Malcolm's vocabulary. It was my first broken bone and first real injury.

The only upside was that the last round of the European championship wasn't until the end of September, so I'd have plenty of time to recover. As for the world championship?

Well, with just two rounds to go, I'm afraid that was it for me in 1994. The eventual winner was Jordi Tarrés, making it his sixth title.

By the time we got to Germany, which is where the final European championship round took place, I was in good form, having recently taken part in the Trials des Nations alongside Dougie, Steve Saunders and Steve 'Showtime' Colley. They used to call Steve 'Showtime' because he was flamboyant and used to play up to the crowd at indoor events. Somebody once called me 'Showtime Jarvis', but I assume they were taking the piss. For the sake of the team, Steve and I put our egos to one side for a bit and I think his confidence helped fuel our motivation.

In those days the Spanish team, which consisted of Jordi Tarrés, Marc Colomer, Joan Pons and Angel Garcia, were streets ahead of everyone else, so we weren't expected to win. Sure enough, the Spaniards ended up winning comfortably in the end, and although we were unable to seriously challenge them, we did manage to beat a very strong Italian team that included Diego Bosis, Donato Miglio, Dario Re Delle Gandine and Piero Sembenini to the runner's-up position. We'd get our revenge on the Spanish team one day, but for now with Dougie, Steve and me being just teenagers it was men against boys really. Give us a few more years. Then we'd see.

On top of the success here, I'd recently finished a very respectable fifth in the 1994 British Trials championship and had also competed in the Australian Trials championship, which I'd actually won. This particular competition had lasted just a weekend and although it wasn't the first time I'd been abroad it was the first time I'd been on a plane. I flew there on my own and I remember Malcolm explaining to me where I had to go at the airport. Fortunately the importer was picking me up, and despite my age and inexperience I don't remember being especially scared or intimidated, either by the trip or the competition. The only person I knew out there was Stefan Merriman, who was also competing in the championship and fortunately he came second!

Don't get me wrong, the standard out there was not what it was in places like Spain, France or the UK, but a win's a win, and it was a fantastic experience. I was still only nineteen years old, so to go to the other side of the world and compete in a national championship in a professional sport – and win – was something that most people could only dream of.

Despite all that, the extent of my ambitions were slightly loftier than the Australian championship, and when I set off on the first section on that final round in Germany I was probably more confident than I ever had been in my life. I wasn't a winner yet – not in the Jordi Tarrés sense of the word – but at least I knew what it felt like to come out on top. With every other result and situation I'd experienced thrown into the mix, such as my relationship with Malcolm and good performance at the Trials des Nations, I could almost describe myself as being an old head on young shoulders. I wasn't complacent, though, as I keep on saying. In fact the last time I'd been complacent was when David Page had beaten me on home soil at a round of the Youth Championship. What a lesson that was! Since then, I've always treated my opponents with the utmost respect, and the same goes for whichever course or section I'm riding.

I may be procrastinating here slightly for the simple reason that I'd rather not get on to the result! I suppose that gives it away, doesn't it? Yes, I'm afraid I lost. The first few sections in Germany went exactly as I'd hoped, and at the halfway point it was all going according to plan. Then, on the second lap I made one big mistake and unfortunately there was no way of pulling it back. It was actually quite an easy Trial and I was absolutely gutted. Malcolm was too, I could tell he was pissed off. And so he should have been. I think I'd led the championship from the second round, so to lose it on the second to last section of the last round was pretty devastating.

A young Spanish rider called Jose Antonio Benitez won the championship, and what makes it worse is that he didn't do a thing after this. He just disappeared! Had he gone on to become a world champion, I'd have felt better, but he went on to open a motorbike shop in Spain. The fact is, the sport of Trials was becoming increasingly difficult and promising young riders with just as much talent as me were starting to disappear as quickly as they arrived.

Immediately after the round, I could only think about what might have been, and that whatever I'd achieved before was now meaningless. In my head, at least. I was just devastated. That was my last chance to compete at the Europeans as next year I'd be too old so from now on it would just be the worlds.

I've already said that nobody remembers second, and that's so true. Especially to a professional sportsperson. I might only have won two rounds in the 1994 European champion-ship and the Australian championship, but the fact is I'd got that winning feeling again, and I desperately wanted more. You'll probably read this in a thousand sporting memoirs or autobiographies, but winning *is* addictive. Not romantically. Truly. Regardless of whether you're a table tennis player or a Trials rider, if you don't ache every time you don't win, especially at the start of your career, you shouldn't be doing it. It's as simple as that. The trouble is, with that ache comes a whole host of other emotions, and it can be overwhelming at times.

When I say I was devastated, I don't mean in a cry-baby kind of way. I was upset, of course I was, but I was also angry with myself.

To ruin an opportunity that big and at such an early stage in my career was hard to take, and it took me a long time to get over it. I'm not sure it affected any future performances, though. Malcolm saw to that. He obviously knew how upset I was, but in his eyes it was up to me to use the result – and the experience of winning a few rounds – as a springboard to getting better. How right he was. Not that he said it in so many words. It was often what Malcolm didn't say that made the most noise. With me, at least. I'd just have to pick myself up and plough on, as per usual. The important thing was to try and keep progressing. No matter how slow it was.

Right On my very first bike that Dad found at the tip. As you can tell, I'm always happiest on two wheels.

Below First audience? Showing off in front of neighbours Joanna and Tony Stingemore.

Above A very little me on the Honda TLM.

Left Having fun on my Fantic. This might have been during an episode of *Junior Kick Start*.

Right Everybody
had a Yamaha TY80
including me.

Below On my TY80
in the woods behind
home. It's where I
learned my craft.

Left Competing at an arena trial with Kent Youth Trials Club, aged about eleven.

Below With my elder brother, Barry, alongside some of my first trophies.

Top right Collecting a Kick Start for winning . . . *Junior Kick Start!* This was my first series win in 1989. Thirty years on, it's still something I get asked about a lot.

Below right The infamous Big Bertha, parked outside our home in the early 1990s. David Jones, the man who gave us the van, very kindly paid to have my picture put on the side.

Left Dad, me and Malcolm – close friend, mentor and minder – after my first win in the World Outdoor Trials Championship in July 2001. A proud, proud moment.

Below left Attacking the Welsh rockery on my Scorpa.

Right Holding aloft the winner's trophy for the Scott Trial in 2008.

Below Riding for Husaberg in the early days of Hard Enduro. So much has changed since then.

Right Lining up alongside my old rival Dougie Lampkin at a Hard Enduro race in 2008.

Below Winning my last Scott Trial in 2009. Last one so far, that is!

6

I finished fourteenth in the 1994 world championship. Given the fact I'd missed the last two rounds that wasn't too bad, and despite my German cock-up, I was looking forward to 1995.

With no European championship on the cards my sights were firmly set on the worlds again, and at the first round in Luxembourg I managed to achieve one of the goals I'd set myself the previous year – to finish in the top ten at a round of the world championship. This not only represented the progress I'd made, which had been slow but steady, but also my ability to manage my expectations, which was essential. I'd made a top-ten finish a priority in 1994 and when that hadn't happened, through no fault of my own, I'd carried the ambition through to the following year. When I arrived in Luxembourg, a top-ten finish was all I could think about, and looking back it was definitely one of my better days in the sport of Trials. I think Malcolm may even have smiled again, and when we turned up for round two, at Hawkstone Park, we were hoping for a repeat show.

While I was researching this period, I came across a report on the 1995 Hawkstone Park round on YouTube, but I've been in two minds as to whether I should tell you what I saw. In the interests of accuracy – and the fact that I don't remember much – I may as well go ahead. It's a story of tragedy and triumph in a way: the tragedies being mechanical and, believe it or not, sartorial, and the triumph being the result. Confused? You will be. Let me try and explain.

Because I was now a professional Trials rider I obviously had to dress like one, and prior to the 1995 season it had been suggested by some sick individual that I might like to wear a one-piece Lycra riding suit. One-piece riding suits had been all the rage since Jordi Tarrés had started wearing one but I wasn't a fan. That's not the worst of it, though, as the colour of this thing was awful. Or should I say, colours. It was purple mainly, but at times it merged into pink, yellow, blue and orange. It was horrendous! These Lycra suits were new at the time, and at some point during the video report it's mentioned that I'm wearing one. I wish I hadn't been. I remember Rhoda telling me to try it on, and it took her ages to coax me out of the caravan.

'Come on Graham. Let's have a look at you.'

'No! I look like a right tit.'

'I bet you don't. Oh, come on Graham.'

'Alright then. I'll come out.'

'Oh dear...'

Shortly before I went out on the first round I was interviewed for the cameras and spectators, and the man with the mic makes reference to me having had 'the Rathmell team haircut'. This immediately took me back to the day itself, or should I say the day before. I'd been to have my hair cut and because I'd had it cut short – in fact, I think I'd had it shaved – it was compared by some people to Malcolm's haircut, which is, to put it politely, slightly lacking in something. Namely, hair. It became known as the Rathmell Team Haircut, and the last thing I did before going out on the round at Hawkstone Park was to take off my helmet and show my hair to the crowd, which got a few laughs. I still had more than Malcolm did. Obviously.

At the tenth section, just as I was attempting to jump up a step, my throttle cable broke. I nosedived the step but managed to bounce back, feet up. The crowd went wild but there was nothing I could do. I don't remember this, but when Malcolm asks me what's wrong the YouTube video clearly shows that I use a word beginning with the letter 'F' before taking a hand off my handlebars and putting it over my mouth. I can obviously become frustrated when things aren't going my way – who can't – and the same thing had happened twice to me in Luxembourg, so no wonder I was annoyed. I suppose everybody suffers bits of bad luck like that, but the reason I took it so badly that time was because it cost me points.

Despite the colourful Lycra, the dodgy haircut and the throttle cable, I still managed to finish ninth at Hawkstone Park, so all in all it was a good weekend. After all the hard work I'd put in, and the disappointments I'd suffered, I felt as though I deserved it.

Unfortunately I wasn't able to maintain that early form and the world championship, on the whole, was something of a disappointment that year. I did manage one more top-ten finish – a ninth in muddy Poland – but the rest of my performances, while mainly in the points, were all quite forgettable.

I managed to finish third in the British championship behind Steve Colley, who eventually won it, and Dougie. I'd still have liked to win, of course, but the podium there and another second at the 1995 Trials des Nations alongside Dougie, Steve Colley and Steve Saunders, stopped me from becoming too depressed.

It was about this time that I started receiving invitations to appear at some more indoor Trials which resulted in some pretty entertaining crashes. Some of the sections were crazily high and a lot of confidence was required to attempt them. Because I was the lowest ranked I had to go first, and I don't mind admitting that I was terrified. There were massive leaps and with nothing like this to practise on at home I just had to launch myself and hope for the best. I forget how many times I crashed but it was over a dozen. One time I landed on my wrist and I remember I couldn't change gear in the van so I had to use my opposite hand all the way home.

To be honest I was never really keen on the indoor stuff. For a start the crowds were massive, and that alone used to terrify me. A hundred people in a field was bad enough, so riding into an arena with five or ten thousand spectators was almost too much to bear. My indoor highlight was probably Birmingham 1997 which I won. There were only a few hundred spectators though, so perhaps that was it? The other thing I don't like about indoor Trials is that they're ... indoors! I much preferred riding outdoors in Trials, so I always considered the world indoor championship, which you obviously have to compete in if you're a professional as it's so important, to be a bit of a necessary evil.

90

I actually remember getting booed in Spain once. It was during the Trial des Nations indoor competition, and whenever one of the British riders did well the Spanish crowd would start booing and shouting what I assume were rude words. The atmosphere was like a bullfight and regardless of my discomfort during the outdoor Trials at home it made me appreciate the fans, as ultimately they just want to see you do well, whoever you are. Well, most of the time. It was a struggle, though, and I never got used to the crowds. Nothing's straightforward with me, I'm afraid.

My ambition for 1996, in addition to winning the national lottery and buying a farm miles away from anywhere with plenty of room to ride, was to finish in the top ten of the outdoor world championship. My previous ambition of finishing in the top ten of a round had been achieved, so it was time to set my sights a bit higher. The year before had been a bit of a dead loss, or at least that's how it felt, and I think Malcolm was also getting a bit frustrated as I'd had two years finishing fourteenth. There was a lot of talent coming through at the time, as well as the existing crowd, and one way or another we had to start making things happen.

Unlike 1995, 1996 got off to a bit of a mixed start and by the middle of April I'd managed a fourth in the first round of the indoor championship and a sixteenth in the first round of the outdoor. That was a bit weird. I still hated indoor Trials at the time but seemed to be showing more progress than I was in the outdoor. Fourth, though. That was a heck of an effort and by the second round of the outdoor championship, which was again held at Hawkstone Park, I'd managed to sort myself out and finished fifth. This was a massive achievement, and it was brought into perspective when I looked at the final leader board. I'd finished above Jordi Tarrés. The man had dominated Trials for donkey's years – certainly since I'd started – and regardless of Dougie's talent and potential Jordi was still the sport's biggest name. It was obviously only symbolic really but as far as my confidence and motivation were concerned I'd just beaten a multiple world champion, and in the remaining eight rounds of the 1996 outdoor world championship I posted a further five top-ten finishes, which, after the final round, left me in ninth position. I'd done it! I'd managed to finish in the top ten. I couldn't quite match it in the indoor world championship, but I had some good results and ended up finishing twelfth.

Given the above, I suppose you could say that I'd now made it as a professional Trials rider, although financially I was still only scraping by. I still had Big Bertha for transport and was still living with Malcolm and Rhoda, so at the end of the day I didn't have too much to complain about.

But as proud as I was – and am – of my achievements in the outdoor and indoor world championships, the highlight for me in 1996 was winning the legendary Scott Trial.

The Scott was, and is, different to any other Trial on earth. Eighty-four miles, seventy-six sections – all timed and observed – and you get a penalty point for every minute you finish behind the fastest rider which is added to the marks you lost in the sections.

The Trial was started back in 1914 when a man called Alfred Scott, inventor and founder of the Scott Motorcycle Company, who made bikes from the turn of the century until the late 1960s, challenged some of his workers at the factory to ride from there through the Yorkshire Dales to a village near Grassington called Burnsall. Of the fourteen riders Scott persuaded to accept his challenge only nine finished so this could have been the first ever Hard Enduro!

Despite his intentions to repeat the event the following year Alfred Scott was unable to because of the outbreak of the First World War. After reintroducing the Trial in 1919 Scott continued to stage the event until his death in 1923, after which his factory workers, who were now as dedicated to the event as he had been, took over running it until 1926. After that the Bradford and District Motor Club took control of the Scott Trial and moved the start and finish to a village called Blubberhouses, which is about fifteen miles away from where I now live in Ripon. In 1938 the land where the Trial was being staged was bought by the Leeds Waterworks Authority, who decided not to allow the Trial to continue, the miserable sods. After that the Trial was moved to Swainby, which is on the north-western corner of the North York Moors National Park in Cleveland and management of the event was taken over by the Middlesbrough and Stockton Motor Clubs. In 1950 the Scott Trial was moved to Swaledale, which is in the Yorkshire Dales National Park, and it has remained there to this day. It starts and finishes in a town called Reeth and is run by the Richmond Motor Club.

I first competed in the Scott Trial in 1992, and I have to admit that I didn't really get the gist of it at first. It never really meant that much to us southerners, and because all the other riders seemed to be northerners I just kept my head down that first year and tried to complete the course at an easy pace. I remember my hands cramping up at one point and I was in agony for about an hour. I'd never experienced that kind of pain before, but even so by the end of the Trial I was hooked. As soon as I'd got to grips with what I was supposed to be doing, of course.

It was actually Malcolm who first told me to get a move on. During his glory years he'd set the fastest time three years running at the Scott, and seeing me plodding along must have offended him. I didn't know him that well at the time, but after spotting me he shouted something along the lines of, 'You do realise this is a bloody time Trial, don't you? Get a bloody move on, lad!'

The reason the Scott Trial is so special to me is two-fold really. First, it was Malcolm's favourite Trial and that alone made it very important to me. Over the last few years I'd probably spent more time with him than anyone else in the world and although we'd had the occasional cross word we'd become quite close. Or as close as a couple of miserable sods like us can be.

Malcolm had won the Scott six times. Only the great Sammy Miller had won it as many times as him, and I'm pretty sure that despite Malcolm winning everything there was to win back then he considered his success at the Scott to be his biggest achievement. And rightly so.

The other reason the Scott Trial is so important to me is that it catalysed my transition from Trials to Hard Enduro, although this only became apparent much later. Riding quickly on a single track suited me down to the ground and I always enjoyed the speed element of the Scott far more than I did the sections. In hindsight, it was very much like a Hard Enduro, but because it was the only speed event on the calendar, it remained nothing more than a novelty.

Subsequently, the Scott Trial also became my favourite event, and that first win in 1996 is one of the proudest moments of my Trials career. It was for Malcolm, that one, and over the years I think preparing for it, competing in it and winning it occasionally cemented our relationship.

Despite the speed of the Scott Trial being the biggest attraction, it has been my undoing occasionally and it's taught me some invaluable lessons. During one of the early Scott Trials I competed in I remember going flat out and after passing a rider in some long grass I hit a rock, somersaulted, and broke my front wheel. I limped to the next stop with all kinds of parts hanging from the bike and luckily Malcolm was there to help me fix it. The lesson was obviously to exercise caution in long grass. There could be anything in there!

I was about twenty minutes behind on time when I crashed, and apparently when my dad found out he told Rhoda he was off home.

'But you can't go now,' said Rhoda.

'I can,' he replied. 'He's not going to win now.'

To be fair to Dad he's always been extremely supportive. I knew exactly where he was coming from though, and I'd have been the same. Rhoda managed to persuade him to stay in the end, and it's a good job he did, as I ended up coming second.

Every time I eased off a bit, Malcolm would say, 'Come on, boy. You're slacking,' and I'd wake up and go up a gear. I think he taught me to ride the Scott exactly the same way he'd done it and it obviously paid dividends.

After 1996, the Scott Trial became almost like an obsession

for me, and from then on it was the only Trial on the calendar that I really looked forward to. It was the closest I came to being excited! Sod Christmas, I'm waiting for the Scott. People who take it seriously, like me, often train specifically for the Scott Trial, and it's advisable to do so. Because of the intensity, it requires a different level of fitness, and if you don't train and prepare yourself properly, you're going to be in trouble. The best place to train for the Scott Trial – and for the Scottish Six Days Trial, if you're based in Yorkshire – is on some land near Kettlewell in North Yorkshire. It's owned by an old Trials legend called Bill Wilkinson and about a month before the Trial takes place all the serious contenders – or the contenders who take it seriously – will ask Bill if they can take their bikes up there. That's the place to go. It's a mile-long rocky stream bed and it's relentless. I used to go up and down it until I couldn't physically hang on!

In 2001 it rained the entire week leading up to the Scott Trial, and during the Trial itself. This meant the conditions were far from ideal, even for me. There are a few river crossings included in the Scott and because of the rain they were a lot wider than usual. I was in the lead when I came across the first one and it was massively swollen. *What the hell am I going to do here?*, I thought. After ruling out jumping, I remembered that Malcolm had once told me that they used to carry their bikes across in his day, so I decided to go in and see how deep it was. Instead of it being up to my waist it was up to my neck. What's more, the river was moving at quite a pace and after swimming out to the middle I realised I was moving down the river very quickly. Carry a bike across? I couldn't even get myself across!

After swimming back towards the bank as quickly as I could the lad I was riding with, Andy Huddlestone, managed to grab hold of me and help me out. It was touch and go, though, and had he not been there I would have been in trouble. Needless to say I was absolutely freezing!

'What should we do now?' I asked Andy.

'May as well walk down the river to see if we can find a shallower bit.'

After walking a few hundred yards we managed to find a shallower bit but carrying our bikes across was still hard going and by the time we reached the other side they were still full of water. We later found out that there was a bridge about half a mile away! There were only six riders who did the whole course that year.

There used to be an indoor event that took place the same time as the Scott Trial on the island of Réunion, and it was quite a big thing. Dougie would ride it sometimes and one year I thought about doing the same. The prize money was good, which is often the way with the indoor Trials, so I went to see the boss.

'Malcolm,' I said, 'I was thinking about riding on the island of Réunion this year, and I wondered what you thought?'

'Next question?'

I didn't ask again. The Scott was sacred.

One of the things that enabled me to win the Scott Trial was a change in my preparation that I'd first incorporated into my routine in 1995. It definitely gave me the edge, although at the time I didn't think so. About two weeks before the Trial Malcolm said completely out of the blue, 'Right then, boy. You're going to spend the whole of next week preparing your bike for the Scott.'

'How do you mean?' I asked.

'You're not going to ride your bike at all. You're just going to work on it and make sure it's right. You don't do that nearly enough before a Trial, so this is where you start.'

As Malcolm spoke I remember experiencing a slight surge of panic, and had I been a little bit braver I'd have protested loudly. I lived for riding motorbikes, and the thought of not doing so the week before the Scott seemed unfair and foolhardy. I did have a whinge to Malcolm, I think, but I ultimately did as I was told. To be fair, this was after some minor bike issues at previous Scott Trials.

The following Saturday, which was exactly a week before the Trial, I started working on my bike, and by the following Friday I understood exactly why Malcolm had made me do it. The Scott Trial is long, fast and unforgiving, and anything can happen on the way. Subsequently, unless you know your bike inside out, you're not giving yourself the best chance of winning because you can make repairs along the way. Also, because I hadn't ridden for the best part of a week I was like a coiled spring and couldn't wait to start.

Something else that Malcolm started doing around this time, which was also essential for my progression, although more generally, was forcing me to practise with riders who were better than me, as opposed to just riders I felt comfortable with. It was all to do with taking me out of my comfort zone, I suppose, and learning from the best, although I don't mind admitting that I was dead against the idea at first.

I remember Malcolm suggesting it one day. 'I think you should go and practise with Jordi Tarrés,' he said.

'Why?' I replied.

'Because he's the best Trials rider in the world and you might learn a thing or two!'

Honestly. I don't know where Malcolm got the patience.

He was absolutely right, of course; Mart Lampkin had already been doing exactly the same thing with Dougie. The difference was that as opposed to arriving and introducing yourself to everybody like Dougie probably did, I'd just arrive, say nothing and try and blend into the background. In all seriousness, I found it very, very hard putting myself in that situation, as it was the opposite of what came naturally to me. It did get better as I got to know some of the other riders, and as soon as I was on my bike I was OK. I just found it difficult getting there. How much difference this all made is difficult to gauge exactly, but it definitely improved my chances. Providing it doesn't overwhelm you, riding with people of that calibre – in fact, just being around them – rubs off on you.

With regards to me not riding the week before the Scott and working on my bike, that was like an extreme version of what Malcolm had taught me at the start of our time working together, and although it was difficult it made me respect my bike even more. I think it's part of the mental preparation as I actually found it therapeutic 'fettling' my bike before a Trial.

The above was all based around a saying that Malcolm used to quote to me which, I think, was called the Six Ps: *Piss Poor Planning results in Piss Poor Performance*. Something else I remember Malcolm saying was, 'The things that need doing before a Trial make up fifty per cent of your chances of winning the Trial.' I got that one immediately. He's a clever bloke, that Malcolm Rathmell.

The thing is, as I became more proficient at this kind of meticulous preparation I started to worry about the tiniest things, and Malcolm and his mechanic Sheldon had a very novel way of dealing with it. I've since learned that most riders go through this, but after working on my bike all week, the night before a Trial I'd convince myself that there was something wrong with, for instance, the clutch.

'It just doesn't feel right,' I'd announce.

'Give it here,' Sheldon would say, and then he'd take it into the workshop. Two minutes later he'd emerge with the bike and say it was fixed. I never asked what he'd done or what he thought was wrong with it, but it always seemed fine after that.

In truth, Sheldon hadn't done anything to the bike, as there was absolutely nothing wrong with it. Had he tried telling me that, however, I'd never have believed him, and my obsession, which is what it was, would have festered and I'd have lost concentration. What Sheldon did was obviously a placebo, and over the years I think we've all been prescribed one or two. Apparently even Malcolm used to go to his boss complaining about this and that, and after someone pretended to mend it, he'd ride off a happy man.

Something else that's unique about the Scott Trial is the presentation ceremony. Nobody knows the results until they're announced at the ceremony, which takes place a few hours after the Trial has finished, and they're always read out in reverse order. For somebody who is averse to presentation ceremonies – and that's putting it mildly – this one's almost bearable, and the first time I heard my name read out last, which meant I'd won, I wasn't trying to find the exit, which was strange. I rather like winning the Scott.

When I was a kid my dad used to have to literally drag me to the presentation ceremonies. I always used to protest, but he was having none of it. 'You can't not turn up to the presentation ceremony, Graham,' he used to say to me.

'Why not?'

'It just isn't done.'

'I don't care,' I'd say walking to my room. 'I don't want to go.'

'You're going and that's final, young man,' Dad would shout finally. 'Now, get your coat on!'

We used to go through the same thing every time I won something, and the more I won the less I wanted to go.

The thing is, the prospect of winning an award or a cup for riding a motorbike was, and is, fantastic. It was the prospect of having to collect the bloody thing that bothered me. It's hardly any different these days, to be honest. In fact, I think the Scott Trial stands alone in that respect as it's the only one I look forward to collecting.

If I win a race, I think, *Brilliant. Well done!* Then I see the podium and I think, *Oh God! Really? Can't I just go home?* It's not that I don't appreciate the effort that everyone goes to. I just find it a bit uncomfortable. Although a lot less than I used to. The vast majority of people obviously don't get it. Or me.

One of my nicknames is 'G-Force Jarvis', but another one is 'Grim' or 'Grimbo'! The definition of grim is 'very serious or gloomy', so it's really only half right. I might get a bit gloomy from time to time, but I'm not serious. The name seems to have caught on somewhat, and now every year a group of American Hard Enduro enthusiasts organise an event called the Grimpossible Challenge in which I demonstrate a series of challenges on my bike before the enthusiasts try and copy me. That's not grim, surely? If anything, it's the opposite!

As I just said, presentation ceremonies are actually becoming easier as I get older. I realised many years ago that the whole sponsorship thing is essential these days, and if you're not prepared to get up onto a podium, shake a few hands and smile for ten minutes before answering a few questions, then you're in danger of damaging the sport you're supposed to love, and that's madness. It's not much to ask.

In the early days I honestly think I was allergic to microphones. When I saw one, I'd freeze and start breathing heavily. It was like being stung by something. I was also known as 'Mr Yes or No' to some of the journalists on the circuit (yet another nickname) because that was the extent of my answers.

'Did you find that difficult today, Graham? That last section was a killer.'

'Yes.'

'Do you think you'll do anything differently tomorrow?'

'No.'

'Thanks, Graham. Fascinating as always!'

'Pleasure.'

Incidentally, I might not have said much, but it didn't matter whether I was collecting a trophy or talking to a journalist, I was always polite. If I hadn't been my mum would have killed me!

The last year I won the Scott Trial, in 2009, was probably the most unexpected win of my career, and I've had a few of them! James Dabill was a few minutes in front of me when all of a sudden I got some muck in my carburettor and came to a halt. It took me ages to get the bike started again and by the time I did I was so far behind James that Malcolm, Rhoda and I thought it would be impossible for me to catch him. I think I had something like fourteen time marks against me in all, so when we turned up to the presentation ceremony after the Trial we were all a bit flat. When my name wasn't read out for third position I thought that was it and was ready to congratulate James. Then, when they read out second, I couldn't believe it. 'In second place, James Dabill,' said the MC. Who the bloody hell's got first then, I wondered, and I could tell by the atmosphere in the hall that everyone else was thinking exactly the same.

'And in first place, Graham Jarvis!'

At first I thought there must have been some mistake, but I didn't say anything. The entire room was in shock, but nobody more than me. It was two years since I'd ridden Trials and with James Dabill being in the top ten in the world at the time I wasn't considered to be in with a chance. What a night that was. To win the Scott Trial nine times and become its most successful rider was – and is – a big old achievement. I will have another go one day. I might be in a wheelchair, though!

I finished the 1997 outdoor world championship in sixth position for the second year running. There'd been a couple of podiums along the way, and plenty of top ten finishes, but it just wasn't good enough. Even finishing fifth in the indoor world championship and first at the Trials des Nations couldn't put a positive spin on it.

One of the things that put me on a downer was that Dougie had won both the indoor and outdoor world championships that year, not to mention the British championship. He'd been making great progress year after year and had obviously allowed himself to dream about becoming world champion, and then gone on and achieved his goal. For some reason I thought that particular accolade was out of my grasp, yet it was the only one I really wanted. I'd had to set my sights lower than Dougie in recent years because I didn't have the support he did, but now I'd made it into the top ten where else was there to aim for other than the top? I was obviously far too young to consolidate my position and forget about my ambitions, so what else was I supposed to do?

By the end of the year, and for the first time in my life, I started asking myself if I should be looking for something else, and not because I didn't want to ride a bike anymore. On the contrary. I wanted to do nothing else! The biggest question was, if I couldn't challenge competitively for the biggest prize of all, what was the point? I'd finished 14th, 9th and 9th in the previous three years so 1998 would be a make or break year.

If I had my time again, I would probably have moved into Enduro a lot earlier, and who knows where that could have led? It was definitely more suited to my character and style of riding, although there's no guarantee I'd have been a success. In fact, I could have been crap. The grass isn't always greener, after all, and as much as I know now about Enduro and Hard Enduro, there could have been aspects to the sport back then that wouldn't have suited me. Who knows?

What I had to try and do again was concentrate on the positives, work hard and see where the world took me. Providing I carried on competing in the world championship, that was going to be places like Spain, the USA, Japan, San Marino, the Czech Republic, Germany, France, Andorra, Finland and Norway.

Come to think of it, it wasn't a bad life for a twenty-two-year-old.

7

If it hadn't been for Malcolm and Rhoda, I probably would have left Trials at that early stage in my career. Then again, if it hadn't been for them, I would never have got this far in the first place, so it was only right that they were one of the main reasons for me staying in the sport. I obviously had my own ambitions, but I also wanted to pay them back for all the help, care and investment they'd bestowed on me, and the only way I could do that was by working hard and trying my very best.

Going back a bit further, if it hadn't been for all the help and support Mum and Dad gave me I wouldn't have met Malcolm and Rhoda, so they're just as much to blame! They always used to stay in the background, though, and would leave me and Malcolm to get on with it. According to Rhoda, who remembers everything, Mart Lampkin always used to ask where my dad was at Trials and he'd always be on his own somewhere. I think he felt privileged that Malcolm was looking after me and instead of getting involved like a lot of parents would have he just left us to it. From my point of view, that was probably for the best as if I'd had Dad and

Malcolm in close proximity – and the spectators, of course – I'm not sure how I'd have coped. Just knowing he was there – and Mum, a lot of the time – was more than enough for me.

One year, while we were in America for the outdoor championship, he and Mum, who's called Ann, just turned up one day right out of the blue. They hadn't said that they were coming, so I obviously wasn't expecting to see them. Then, all of a sudden, there they were!

'Hello, Graham,' Dad said in a very matter-of-fact way. 'How're you getting on?'

I couldn't believe it, and neither could Malcolm or Rhoda.

'Where the hell did you spring from?' I asked.

'We landed about an hour ago.'

'From where?'

'England, of course!'

'You never said you were coming.'

'Oh, we just decided to come along.'

'What, to America?'

'Yeah, why not?'

That sums my parents up. Unpredictable but brilliant.

My dad ended up becoming part of the team in a way, as even though he'd never ridden before he would watch the early riders sometimes and then report back to Malcolm about which lines had worked and which hadn't. He didn't take it upon himself to do that. Malcolm asked him to. I think he was surprised at first but he'd been watching Trials for so many years and his experience had to count for something. He was very much part of the team.

To be fair to Mum, she got involved quite a bit too, and her role was even more essential than Dad's. Whenever we came back from a world championship round, Mum would have beers waiting for Malcolm, Dad and Mart Lampkin. Not for me. I had to make do with orange juice.

At the end of every season, usually on the way home from the last round of the outdoor world championship, Malcolm would go through what I needed to do to progress the following year, and naturally I took every word as gospel. The previous year he'd mentioned my balance, so that's one of the things I'd worked on over the winter. Malcolm and Rhoda had heard that Jordi Tarrés used to walk along fences to improve his balance and when they told me that my ears immediately pricked up. If it was good enough for Jordi, it was good enough for me. The following morning Rhoda got the shock of her life when she opened her bedroom curtains. Instead of looking out on her garden and a few birds, she also saw me wobbling along her garden fence. 'Malcolm, come and have a look at what Graham's doing now.' I think she thought I'd lost the plot. Perhaps I had?

A few weeks later I went to Belgium with Malcolm and Rhoda's nephew, Sam, and, after seeing a very long fence somewhere he challenged me to walk it. Unfortunately, I have a big problem turning down challenges and I spent hours trying to clear the thing. Just when I thought I had the better of it I fell arse over tit and I ended up needing about five stitches in my chin. My balance had definitely improved, though.

In hindsight, I wish I'd gone to Malcolm and Rhoda's much sooner, as they could have done wonders with my confidence if they'd got me at a far more formative age.

I always assumed that Malcolm and Rhoda had started to lose faith in me at the end of 1997, and for no other reason than I'd started to lose faith in myself. I thought I'd let them down, and presumed they felt the same. After having a chat with Rhoda over Christmas it appears I was wrong, and the only person who was doubting me was me. It's funny what the mind makes up.

What helped to turn me around, apart from the continued support of Malcolm and Rhoda and Mum and Dad, was the ability to motivate myself a bit, and at the end of 1997 I gave myself a proper kick up the arse. I was travelling all over the world doing something I loved – and I was getting paid for it. What other twenty-two-year-olds could say that? More importantly, though, I'd just finished in the top ten of the world championship for the second year running and had the support and, dare I say, the talent, to do even better. That's what I started to tell myself, and that's what I started to believe. Well, I tried.

At the beginning of 1998 I competed in the Sheffield Indoor Trial which is the first round of the world indoor championship. For some reason I'd always struggled at this event but this year I had a bit of confidence about me and took more risks. Subsequently, I managed to get on the podium and afterwards, instead of disappearing quietly like I normally would, I went to the bar and ordered myself a beer and a club sandwich. I remember Dougie and one or two other riders giving me a bit of a strange look when they saw me, but I was starting to chill out a little bit. Until then, to say Graham Jarvis was an intense character would have been a huge understatement!

I think the only thing that was holding us back a bit now was the bike. It was still a bit cumbersome compared to others, but Scorpa had made some improvements during the off-season (they'd managed to shed some weight from the frame, but the engine was still a lump), and I was confident that despite it not being perfect it was better than seventh and eighth. Sure enough, I managed to finish third on the first day at Hawkstone Park and runner-up on the second. This was where I wanted to be. OK, I might not have finished first, but as long as I was in the top three, or thereabouts, I was sure I'd stand a chance of getting to the top spot occasionally and from there – well, who knows?

At the following round, in San Marino, I repeated my performances at Hawkstone by scoring a third on day one and then a second on day two, so that was four podiums from six starts. Not bad for a lad who, just a few months earlier, had been thinking about giving it up.

The trick was not to get too carried away, and to be honest my performances in the indoor world championship saw to that. That particular competition had started back in January, and when the final round took place in Monte Carlo in March I'd had one podium and a mixture of sixth, seventh and eighth positions. I think I finished sixth overall in the championship, so although I hadn't disgraced myself, I hadn't set the world alight either. Looking at it positively, it was just the leveller I needed.

Next up after the San Marino round was the fabled Scottish Six Days Trial which is undoubtedly the most famous motorcycle Trial in the world and attracts riders and spectators from every continent. Because of its significance, it deserves an introduction.

Running since 1909, the Scottish Six Days Trial is the world's oldest major Trial. As well as testing your riding skills, it also tests your reliability over long distances, with riders completing up to a hundred miles each day over six consecutive days. Each day the riders will take on a combination of coarse moorland, stony tracks and public roads in the best – and often worst – weather the Scottish Highlands has to offer. Let's just say it can be a bit changeable up there!

Riding a hundred miles and negotiating thirty sections a day for six consecutive days is a phenomenal task, and with the best part of three hundred riders taking part every year, anything can happen. This one really does test both man and machine to the absolute max, and the race can either make you or break you.

I entered my first Scottish Six Days Trial in 1992 and finished ninth. The only thing I really remember about the Trial itself is that it rained all week. In fact, I'm not sure if it stopped once during daylight hours. The spectators all thought I was weird because I didn't wear a jacket and quite a few of them told me so. 'You must be bloody mad, Jarvis,' was one popular observation, together with, 'You'll catch your death of cold, lad!' Be that as it may, I just don't like wearing them when I'm riding, so I decided to risk getting hypothermia and remain comfortable instead. Ninth wasn't a bad effort, even though I do say so myself, and I got to spend eight hours a day on my bike so I loved every minute.

My strategy at the Scottish Six Days Trial was always to hang back so I would never be the first rider into a section. There were three reasons for this. First, there'd always be more people watching you if you were first in and to me it was a case of the fewer spectators the better. Second, I don't like riding ahead of people, which probably won't surprise you. And third, the sections usually get a little bit easier later on, so as far as I was concerned it made sense. Patience is something that comes easily to me – I can wait as long as I have to. I did almost get caught out in 1997, and in doing so I almost caused a riot.

A rock had moved on one of the sections, and as I sat back deciding what to do all the other riders started piling through. Every time I was ready to set off again somebody would come along, so I ended up being the very last rider to go through. Because of the time limit it was going to be touch and go as to whether I'd make it back to parc fermé in time, which is the area where the bikes are kept, and the general consensus at the section was that I wouldn't. 'No chance,' they were muttering. I think it was at this point I realised I could ride pretty damn quick with a big dose of adrenaline.

With a bit of a bee in my helmet, I absolutely tore over those moors, and I reached parc fermé with a couple of minutes to spare. So sure were the people who'd doubted me that I wouldn't make it that when they found out I had they started protesting, and some of them demanded an investigation. I don't think I'd ever been accused of cheating before, but to be honest it didn't bother me. They must have thought I'd tampered with my timecard or something and when they found out that I hadn't and that I'd been telling the truth I received one or two begrudging apologies. The majority didn't bother, though.

'But how did you do it?' one of them asked me.

'I was just quick,' I told them.

I finished second overall. It was another sign of what was to come.

The next world championship round after the Scottish Six Days Trial was in the Czech Republic, and despite turning up there with a spring in my step I left feeling slightly deflated. I don't know what I was expecting really, as my success in the competition had been fairly short-lived, but eighth and fifth, which is where I finished, felt like a big step backwards. It wasn't, but that's how it felt.

By the time we got to Germany I was back on the podium again, and I managed to repeat that with a second in France, although I was way down in the second race. By the final round in Norway I was lying fifth behind Steve Colley. Providing I beat him over the two days I'd move up to fourth, so there was a massive amount riding on it. On the first day I finished fifth. I forget where Steve finished, but I remember feeling a huge amount of pressure going into the last day, so he'd obviously done OK. Had it been a couple of years before I'm not sure I'd have coped with the stress, but with my new attitude and the odd beer and club sandwich now and again I felt confident.

The relationship between Malcolm and Rhoda and my parents was also helpful in this situation. Not only did they get on very well with each other, but Mum and Dad respected Malcolm's expertise. Having a united front like that not only made me feel very supported, but it also meant that I only had one voice telling me what to do. Because of Malcolm's experience, that's all I needed.

The battle for fourth position at the 1998 outdoor world championship came down to the last section of the last lap, and I remember thinking that I just had to go for it. Again, had it been 1994 or 1995 I'd have been terrified, but this time I wasn't. I was up for it. Something else that galvanised me was the realisation that all my hard work appeared to be paying off and my experience was coming to the fore. I was making progress.

I actually remember the section. It was a slippery, muddy

rock face that needed full commitment. I cleared it and there is no better feeling. It meant I'd secured fourth, and although I wasn't quite on top of the world in terms of Trials riders, that's exactly how I felt. It was brilliant. A real sense of achievement.

It was about this time that I started seeing Malcolm and Rhoda's daughter Sonya. Having no idea how Malcolm and Rhoda would take the news, we decided to keep it quiet initially, and there was a lot of sneaking about. When they eventually did find out, it didn't go down too well, but they came round in the end. To be fair to Malcolm and Rhoda, I think most people would have been a bit miffed if they found out that somebody who was working for them and somebody they'd looked after for several years was carrying on with their daughter. I know I would. I think they were more worried that it might complicate things, which was a legitimate concern. It didn't, though. In fact, it had the opposite effect on me, as I now had something else in my life other than Trials. I think I'd become a little bit obsessed with it, and because I never thought about anything else – ever – I often found it difficult to relax. Being in a relationship allowed me to do that, and given my age it was about time really. I'd been like a monk on wheels until then. Well, almost.

Towards the end of 1998 I ended up moving out of Malcolm and Rhoda's, although it had nothing to do with me seeing Sonya. I was now twenty-three years old and had been wanting to get on the property ladder for a couple of years. But despite being settled domestically, by the start of 1999 things had started going wrong with Scorpa, and less than a month into the outdoor championship I was without a bike. I'd only recently signed a new contract with them, but in

March they contacted us to say that they wouldn't be able to fulfil it.

The company was owned by two Frenchmen called Joël Domergue and Marc Tessier, and I remember Marc visiting Malcolm's workshop to give us the news. I think he and Joël had fallen out or something, and Marc was going it alone. Although the timing wasn't brilliant, it was actually good news – providing I could find another ride, of course. It may have improved, but the Scorpa still had a Rotax engine and was still heavier than many of the other riders' bikes. Fortunately, Marc had an idea.

Since falling out with Joël had bought the rights in the Bultaco name and had been developing a new bike with a rider called David Cobus. David had recently been injured, so Marc offered me the bike instead. It was still a prototype, but it was like a toy compared to the Scorpa and much more in line with the other bikes on the circuit.

That first round on the Bultaco, which was in Belgium, was the first time the bike had been ridden at an outdoor event. I think David had done some indoor stuff on it, but when it came to outdoor Trials it was an unknown quantity. Fortunately, the bike was OK, and I finished third on the first day which was a massive achievement for everyone. Going forward it was a bit up and down and I still struggled with the big steps and the larger sections. I can't dress it up. I was just too inconsistent.

Until changing to the Bultaco my best result in 1999 had been sixth, so despite being up and down a bit the bike was better than I'd been used to, and I managed to finish fourth again in the championship. Having already secured the same position in the indoor championship and victory at both the

Scott Trial – my fourth in a row – and the Scottish Six Days Trial, it was probably my best year to date. And I was on a bike that was actually improving.

By the turn of the new millennium I was still having problems with consistency. Podium finishes would be followed by finishes outside the top ten and vice versa. It was a nightmare. Then, at Hawkstone Park, in round four of the world championship, disaster struck. I'd managed fourth on the first day, but halfway through the second day, while I was coming out of a section, I jumped off a rock, stuck my foot out and ended up buckling my knee. I did my anterior cruciate ligament, my medial ligament and my cartilage. I did the lot. Unfortunately, instead of stopping immediately and getting help like I should have, I carried on and finished the Trial. The pain was obviously horrendous and when I found out that it might be a career threatening injury and that my knee might never be the same again, I was devastated.

Because of the amount of time riders were taking on sections, the race organisers had introduced a time limit of three minutes per section, and that was definitely a contributing factor in what happened. I was rushing to get to the ends of the sections in time.

I was out for over six months in the end. Until then, the longest I'd gone without riding a bike since the age of about eight was a couple of weeks, so it was torture. It did give me time to reflect on how my career was faring, however, and while I was waiting for my knee to heal I ended up going to see a sports psychologist for the first time. A friend of mine called Roger Tushingham recommended I do it, and he put me in touch with somebody at Sheffield University. Roger used to sail competitively, and he'd used one himself in the past. Despite my reservations, I decided to give it a go. After all, I had nothing else to do!

The main reason I decided to go and see a sports psychologist wasn't my inconsistency, as such. It was my reaction *to* my inconsistency. Sometimes, when I had a bad result, I'd lose the plot. Malcolm had witnessed that in Germany, but it had happened many times before and since then.

The original catalyst for my inconsistency had been a fear of failure. I'm in no doubt about that. Then, once I started losing, things got worse. It was a snowball effect really. A vicious circle.

What the sports psychologist tried to teach me was how not to get caught up in my emotions and to concentrate only on the things I could control. It was easier said than done, of course, but the realisation that I was my own worst enemy and was basically perpetuating my inconsistency by letting myself get so worked up was a revelation. It didn't make the problem go away, but the next time I made a mistake and became emotional about it I just let it all pass and tried my hardest to concentrate on what I needed to do. It was all just common sense.

I also tried hypnotherapy for this problem once, and despite me 'going under', as I think they call it, it didn't make a blind bit of difference. In fact, I was back in the room and on my way home within about fifteen minutes.

In my opinion, professional sports people should leave no stone unturned when it comes to improving their performance. Providing it's legal, of course. My own issues were preventing me from performing to the best of my ability, but even if I hadn't had those issues and was world champion I would still have strived to improve. The injury had given me a newfound appreciation of riding a motorbike and, after what I'd been through, a bad result was easier to accept.

The winter of 2000 to 2001 is when the hard work of my rehabilitation really started, as that's when I got back on a bike. I went over to Spain and trained with a man called Michele Renard. This was the first time I'd ever had a coach, as such, during the winter, but because of my injury it was necessary. I needed somebody to look out for me but also to push me. Malcolm would come to Trials with me, but he never came training, so it was usually just me, myself and I. Michele had worked with Marc Colomer when he was world champion and came highly recommended. Bultaco had been renamed Sherco by this point, and they paid for Michele to help get me back in shape. All we did from the moment we got up until the moment we went to bed was ride. We did cycling in the morning and motorbikes in the afternoon. It was incredibly intense. These days a regime like that would finish me off, but when you're in your early twenties it's a doddle. I was also in Spain, for heaven's sake, so it wasn't a bad little jaunt.

Looking back, the injury was a blessing in disguise, as it enabled me to attend to the psychological side of being a sportsman as opposed to just the physical side. Had I not had the injury I probably wouldn't have met up with Roger when I did, and he'd never have suggested the psychologist. I'd have just carried on regardless, even though my state of mind was something that definitely needed to be addressed.

The first two rounds of the 2001 outdoor world championship were in Spain, which hadn't been my happiest hunting ground, yet I bagged a third on day one and a second on day two. This new attitude of mine was paying dividends and I left Spain on cloud nine.

Despite remaining in the top ten, I didn't get another podium until the French round. This was something else, though, as instead of standing to the left or the right on the podium, I was standing in the middle. After nine years of striving I'd finally won my first world championship round. All of a sudden everything was worthwhile!

Most people would assume that I'd have been elated at winning the round in France, and I was . . . eventually. At first I was in shock, which is understandable. Nine years is a long time, and I was beginning to think it would never happen. Despite enjoying the moment, I started to ask myself what I'd done differently this time. What had changed? I came to the conclusion that I was just a slow learner and was five or six years behind where I should have been. Nothing's really changed in that respect. Mind you, I think it's better to get there later and stay at the top longer than it is to peak at a younger age. There were a lot of young Spanish riders who emerged at the same time as I did in Trials, and the majority of them had already fallen by the wayside.

Before the end of the 2001 championship I won two more rounds, in Andorra and the Czech Republic. It put me in fourth position overall – again – but I was still buzzing. I was now a multiple world-round winner.

8

Finishing 4th in the outdoor championship meant that I once again qualified for a full season of FIM indoor world championship rounds. As a result, I was also invited to compete at some non-championship events in France, and between the two they made for a nice financial boost. Unfortunately, before I could really benefit from any of this I suffered a really bad shoulder injury, so that was it!

It happened during a two-metre jump down from the sleeper section and after falling and landing awkwardly I dislocated my shoulder. I tried continuing but every time I did it would just fall out of my joint. Nice!

While I still didn't particularly enjoy the environment of indoor Trials, I was starting to become more confident in the discipline, and I'd enjoyed some good results in other indoor competitions and had won a few Trials both here and abroad. I even started playing to the crowd occasionally! The psychological help I'd received had definitely helped me cope with the crowds, but I still found it intimidating and difficult to enjoy sometimes.

One of the biggest problems we Brits had when it came to

indoor Trials was training, as there were hardly any facilities in the UK, and it took us a while to catch up with the Spaniards. I never really did though, unfortunately. Dougie had been the world indoor champion several times before I found my feet, but, as I said, I'm always a few years behind.

After having surgery on my shoulder, followed by three months' rest, I was just able to get to the first round of the outdoor world championship, which was still my main focus. By this point I think I'd achieved everything I was going to in the sport. I was certainly capable of winning more, but from now on any additional progress was going to be difficult to achieve and I finally had to try and accept the fact that perhaps Trials wasn't the right sport. It was just too much of an enclosed environment for me which is why the Scott Trial, which is anything but enclosed, suited me so well.

This is all with the benefit of hindsight, of course, but if I had known then what I know now, I may well have been riding in Enduro and enjoying myself much sooner. I've never been a quitter, though, and I can also be incredibly stubborn. A little while ago Rhoda told me that before Martin Lampkin died, Malcolm told him that he'd never known anybody who wanted to ride as much as I did. The thing is, as admirable as things like dogged determination can be at times, it can also prevent you from moving on, and this was a case in point. I also had a very strong team behind me at the time in Malcolm, Rhoda, my parents, Sheldon, who was my mechanic and who also owned a Sherco dealership, and Marc Tessier, and I was, at the end of the day, one of the top Trials riders in the world and the second best that Britain had to offer. I still wanted to be the best, though. I wanted to be world champion. I think deep down everyone knew I had peaked, and not only because there were younger riders coming to the sport with a whole load of new tricks.

With Hard Enduro I still feel nervous from time to time but only before a race. Once I set off that's it. My nerves are gone. In Trials there's an awful lot of stopping and starting and waiting around, which always gave my nerves a chance to regroup. Before I knew it, I was internalising everything again and my mind had taken over. That never happens now. We do obviously stop sometimes in Hard Enduro, but instead of people standing there and judging your performance they're just willing you on. Unless they're fans of Jonny Walker, who is arguably my biggest rival in Hard Enduro. In which case they're willing me off! The point is, we don't have time to get nervous during a race in Hard Enduro. It's adrenalin all the way.

After an indifferent start in Spain, where I got a seventh and a fifth, I then posted a second in Douglas on day one of the British round in the Isle of Man, followed by a sixth. After that I finished anywhere from third to thirteenth throughout the rest of the season, so it was just impossible to predict what I'd do from round to round. People must have thought, *I wonder which Graham Jarvis is going to turn up today?* I wish to hell I'd known, as I might have been able to do something about it.

By the end of the championship I was lying in fifth position, just one mark shy of the future world champion, Adam Raga. It was an OK result considering, but that was just it. I was fed up with doing OK! I couldn't put a positive spin on this if I tried, as all I could think about was the fact that the four riders in front of me, Raga, Albert Cabestany, who was third, Takahisa Fujinami, who was second and Dougie who was the champ, were all younger than I was. I was no longer the future of the sport, and with so much young talent coming through it was questionable as to whether I was still a legitimate contender. Many would say I obviously was, of course, as I was still winning things like the Scott and the odd Trial here and there, but I was no longer the force I had been. There was no question about it. I know Dougie had to work incredibly hard to keep his position at the top, so nobody felt the looming presence of this new bunch of riders more than he did. His work ethic must have been incredible.

Lightening the mood a little bit from being grim to slightly less so, I was able to exact a bit of sweet revenge over the likes of Adam Raga and Albert Cabestany at the Trial des Nations. Trials is right up there when it comes to Spanish pastimes, alongside football and bullfighting, but after a period of dominance in the outdoor world championship, thanks mainly to Jordi Tarrés and Marc Colomer, the titles had suddenly stopped coming. This was obviously down to Dougie, who had dominated the sport since 1997, and it's fair to say that from that point on there'd been little love lost between us and the Spanish riders. They certainly had more strength in depth than we did. After all, the only British riders who could have been categorised as being world class in those days were Dougie, me and Steve Colley, whereas the Spaniards probably had three times the amount.

Great Britain had won the Trials des Nations back in 1999, but the Spanish had managed to wrestle it back the year after. As a nation we Brits pride ourselves on being gracious in defeat, but the same can't always be said of our Spanish counterparts. When we won the Trials des Nations again in 2002 it didn't go down too well with our Iberian friends, and the Spanish team refused to mount the second step of the podium. If memory serves me correctly, they'd lodged two complaints, and both had been speedily rejected by the FIM jury. Amós Bilbao, who is a good guy, filled in for the Spanish team and when Dougie, Steve Colley, Sam Connor and I mounted the centre of the podium I shouted, ''Ave it!' in the direction of the Spaniards who were still sulking. It was totally out of character for me, but my word it was heartfelt. We couldn't believe we'd won, to be honest, as on paper they should have pissed it. I think we just wanted it more on the day. It was bloody sweet, that was. *Gracias, amigos!*

You do occasionally experience a bit of gamesmanship in Trials. According to an online dictionary, the exact definition of gamesmanship is: *the art of winning using questionable measures yet without actually violating the rules.* The first time I experienced it was in Andorra for the 2001 world championship, and the reason I remember it is because it was one of the five world rounds that I won.

I was riding behind Dougie, who had a massive team around him, and when he'd gone on to the next section a member of his entourage would hang around and watch me ride the section at very, very close quarters. The idea was to make me feel nervous at a critical point, but on this occasion it didn't work. In Yorkshire it's called 'old manning' – as in you hang around like an old man – and it used to be commonplace. Needless to say, it wasn't something I appreciated, so the fact that I managed to ignore Amos's attempt and ended up winning was a bit of a two-fingered salute. Up yours, mate! I felt like I'd won against the odds.

*

From a career point of view there are four things I need to tell you about from 2003. Three are special, but one is very special indeed. Let's do it chronologically. Well, more or less.

First up was the Japanese round of the 2003 outdoor world championship which took place in June. After completing a solid winter training programme I was all geared up for the world championship and was hoping to do better than last year and get back into the top four. A fourth and a sixth in Ireland set the ball rolling before a third on day one and a fifth on day two in Luxembourg and a win and a fourth in Germany in round three. When I arrived in Japan for round four I was on a bit of a high, I suppose, and when I realised it was going to be a muddy Trial I started to feel quite confident. Two good results here and I would be into the top three. What a springboard that would be for the rest of the season.

After making a couple of mistakes on day one I only managed second, but on day two I was bang on form and finished first. This was, to date, my best ever round at the world championship, and I went to bed that evening in third place overall. Third place!

The following day, or it could have been the day after, I picked up a very bad case of food poisoning. I was really bad for about a week afterwards with my head down the pan ten times a day, but I didn't feel right for a good couple of months. Actually, that's a bit of an understatement: 'Didn't feel right' translates as a ninth on the opening day in Spain for round six followed by a DNF on day two followed by a trip to hospital where dangerously low blood sugar levels and an irregular heartbeat were diagnosed, with both being traced back to my original bout of food poisoning. I was still undergoing tests as late as September, so God only knows what I'd eaten. Plutonium by the sound of things! It wouldn't have happened with pasta and tinned tomatoes.

The following round in France was rubbish, and despite my results picking up again later on in the year the damage had been done and it was too late. Subsequently, all that momentum I'd built up by securing four podium finishes out of a possible six – not to mention reaching third in the world championship – was lost.

The next three events all happened in October but rather than putting them in date order I'm going to put them in order of significance.

Any Spanish readers might want to turn the page here, but Dougie, Ben Hemingway, Sam Connor and I managed to retain the Trials des Nations. The competition took place in Lavarone, Italy, and I got the best individual score, so it was another sweet one for me. I don't remember there being any argy-bargy this time from the Spanish lot, so there were no shouts of ''Ave it!' or anything like that. Just a handshake and a friendly wink. Well, smug wink, maybe. I also won the Scott Trial again in October 2003, which was my fifth victory.

The undisputed highpoint of my 2003 season was winning the British championship for the very first time. I won all six rounds that year and made sure of my victory in the final round at Kinlochleven, Scotland. Steve Colley was my nearest rival, but he was twenty-three points behind, so it was a very convincing victory. One thing I had in my favour that year was that Dougie didn't take part but when all was said and done I still had to win the thing.

But it was what happened after I won the British

championship that made it really special, and it ended up making two grown men cry. Malcolm had won the British championship six times in his career, and on four of those occasions he'd received a small gold star, which were always more coveted than the usual medals. Whenever he wore a suit, Malcolm would wear these stars with pride, and the likes of Mart Lampkin and Mick Andrews were exactly the same. A few years previously, Malcolm had said to Rhoda that if I ever won the British championship he'd give me one of his stars, and when I finally did he kept to his word.

He and Rhoda had organised an open day that took place a few days after the final round of the championship, and during the day Malcolm brought the proceedings to a halt and made the presentation. I hope he doesn't mind me including this, but Malcolm was crying when he presented me with the gold star, and this set me off too. Rhoda always says that I was overcome because I'd been given the star and Malcolm was overcome because he'd had to give it away!

What an amazing gesture that was, though. Malcolm didn't have to give me the star and the fact that he thought I was deserving of it is one of the biggest compliments I've ever been paid.

Away from the motorbikes, there was one big highlight from 2003, and that was finding out that Sonya was pregnant with twins. Since moving in together life had been good and that news was just the icing on the cake.

Like most expectant parents, I was nervous about what was to come, but this was unlike anything I'd ever experienced in Trials. The prospect of riding over some rocks or through some mud, regardless of the prizemoney involved or how close the spectators, is nothing compared to the prospect of becoming a parent. I was up for it, though – and I was looking forward to it.

Jack and Ellie finally arrived in September 2004 and despite the reality of fatherhood having an even more extreme effect on my nerves than the expectation of it, it was a lot more enjoyable! They were beautiful, but God were they noisy. Like human TY80s!

My only distraction from all this was the fact that the season was still going so it wasn't long before I was back on a bike. The 2004 season so far, had been . . . wait for it . . . inconsistent, and apart from a second in the USA there'd been no real highpoints to report in any of the major competitions.

The only positives, apart from my kids being born, were wins at the Scottish Six Days and the Scott, so it wasn't all doom and gloom. Or grim and grimmer. The Scottish Six Days Trial had taken place in May as usual and the win had given me my hat-trick.

As the oldest and most prestigious event in world Trials, the Scottish Six Days is the one that everybody wants to win. Or at least everybody in the British Isles. That's not to say they don't get foreign riders taking part, because they do. In fact, between 1980 and 1987 overseas riders completely dominated the Trial, and every single winner was from a foreign country. Yrjö Vesterinen was the very first overseas rider to win, in 1980. After that Gilles Burgat won it in 1981, followed by Bernie Schreiber in '82, Toni Gorgot in '83, Thierry Michaud in '84, '85 and '86 – another hat-trick winner – and finally, in 1987, Jordi Tarrés. The only two riders to do it since then are the aforementioned Amós Bilbao and Joan Pons, so the foreign contingent are due another win or six.

They'll have to get past Dougie first, who in recent years has made the Trial his own and has chalked up eleven victories and counting.

A lot of people used to accuse me and Malcolm of communicating via telepathy, and although they were obviously joking there was an element of truth in it. Neither of us said very much, as you know, and because we were on the same wavelength – and because Malcolm had taught me so much of what I knew – we were able to communicate via nods mainly and a few other gestures. We just spoke a different language, that's all.

A lot of people used to compare Malcolm and me to Mart and Dougie, in that you had a former champion minding a younger one, but in truth we were completely different. Dougie and Mart were both quite outgoing, whereas Malcolm and I were both quiet.

Because Mart was so loud you could hear every word of advice he was giving Dougie, and some of that sank in with me. This is no word of a lie, but at one of the world rounds I once heard Mart shout, 'You're on fire, Doug, you're on fire', and I actually thought his bike was on fire! He was shouting it so loudly and with so much conviction I thought it was true. He was a huge character, was Mart.

Somebody once asked me if I would have benefited from having a big character minding for me, and to be honest I don't think I would. For a start, it might have intimidated me a bit, and at the end of the day you've got to ride the bike yourself, so I think I'd have found it a distraction. Malcolm used to give me advice occasionally, but by and large he'd just let me get on with it.

Saying that, Martin did step into the breach on one or two

occasions, so he did actually mind for me. It happened at a couple of indoor events in France that Malcolm couldn't attend, although I don't remember Martin telling me I was on fire! It was good of him to step in though.

One of Rhoda's favourite stories regarding the so-called telepathy between me and Malcolm involves the Scottish Six Days Trial and is probably one of my favourite stories, too, as it encapsulates our personalities and our relationship. I think it was during my first win, so that would have been 1998. We were on the very last section on Ben Nevis, and I had to clean it to win. Malcolm was at the top of the section, and I was at the bottom. Rhoda saw Malcolm nod to me in three different directions, and I nodded back. There were no words. Just nods. We really were the absolute opposite to Mart and Dougie, as if they'd been taking on that section the whole of Scotland would have known how Dougie was going to tackle it.

Winning the Scott was obviously a great way of rounding off the year, and Sonya and the twins were there in our camper van, which was nice. Before we had the kids Sonya had been a mainstay at the Trials – she had been since she was a kid, not surprisingly – but as soon as the twins came along it became more difficult for her to attend. We tried it for a while, but nappies and motorsport competitions don't really mix, and I fully admit that it put a strain on our relationship. For someone who'd been brought up going to Trials every weekend that must have been difficult, especially as she was the only one who was unable to go. Apart from the twins, of course. Even so, Sonya took to motherhood like a duck to water, and while I was away trying desperately to hang on to my career, she did a fabulous job looking after Jack and Ellie.

At the beginning of 2005 I made the difficult decision not to challenge for the world championship again after the end of the current year. In 2004 I'd finished eighth, which, if you discount the year I was injured, was my worst performance since 1997. By then I knew that the writing was on the wall, and I had two choices: either carry on flogging a dead horse for a few years while earning less and less money and moving further down the world rankings while becoming more and more demoralised, or take stock, have a look around and think about doing something else. There was obviously no contest in my mind, and I couldn't wait to get out, but even if I did decide to continue, I'd have had to find a new ride, as Sherco weren't keen on retaining me in the world championship. Quitting something you love is a lot easier when your hand is forced, but for me it merely cemented my decision. I ended up finishing seventh in that final season, and although that was obviously an improvement it didn't change a thing.

Incidentally, by the end of 2005 Sherco had entered the Enduro market with a 450cc 4-stroke. I remember staring at one of the riders' bikes with Malcolm's son, Martin. 'That thing's got a flat tyre,' I said, pointing at the back wheel. 'That's how they run it, to get more grip,' he replied. 'It's got mousse in it.' A mousse being a solid tube that cannot puncture.

Over the next few years I mainly concentrated on the Scott Trial, the Scottish Six Days and the British championship, but in addition to this I also started competing in a few local Enduros and a few Hard Enduros. The British championship in particular was important to Sherco, who were still supporting me for domestic Trials, as it was their big shop window in the UK, and me winning that was probably worth more to them in bike sales than any other competition or Trial. Until this point, Enduro hadn't even entered my head. I asked Martin if I could have a go on a demo bike. I just remember the bike being so heavy as I pushed it out of the workshop. Once I got on it though, I was hooked. I loved the power.

I think the prizemoney for winning a round of the British championship was about £500, which, if I won all six, would earn me the princely sum of £3,000. My contract with Sherco was obviously worth less now that I wasn't competing internationally, so it's fair to say that during my initial few years after breaking free from the international Trials scene and dabbling in Enduro – which at the time paid a lot less than Trials and in my case didn't have a manufacturer contract attached to it – I was not exactly flush with cash. In fact, my wage from Sherco was £8,000, so my earning potential in real terms was about £13,000 all in. I'd have got another paper round if I'd had time.

Between 2006 and 2008, which was the year that I finally retired as a full time Trials rider, I won the Scottish Six Days once, the Scott Trial once and the British Championship twice. So, while I wasn't earning much money or competing at the highest level anymore, I was still doing well domestically.

That last British championship is worth a mention, as it went right down to the wire and was a great way to end my full-time Trials career. By the time we got to the last round, it was a three-way tie between me, Shaun Morris and Michael Brown. I'd wanted to ride in Hard Enduro instead of the British championship this year, but Malcolm had persuaded me to give it one last bash, and I'm so glad I did.

Unfortunately, before we started the final round, which took place in Skipton that September, Shaun Morris suffered a really bad eye injury while tightening his handlebars and it actually finished his career. I think they snapped while he was trying to alter them, and a piece of metal penetrated his eyeball. Shaun was a promising young rider, so it was very sad indeed.

Michael and I were neck-and-neck on points until the final section, and luckily I just managed to edge him out. Mum and Dad were there as well as Malcolm and Rhoda, so it was a great way to round things off: the entire team, all together.

At the end of the day I'd had a good run in Trials, and I figured that as far as the history books were concerned I'd hopefully be remembered as somebody who did OK and finished on a high as opposed to somebody who did OK and then spoiled it all by trying to flog a dead horse for a few years. As well as enjoying every moment (well, almost every moment) the sport had given me a great life and a decent living, and although I'm better known these days as being a Hard Enduro rider I'm always quick to tell people who ask me where it all started.

Quietly, of course.

9

My transition from Trials to Enduro and then Hard Enduro was gradual and started after I began entering more and more local Enduros. Some were a little bit gnarly and they were mostly two and a half hour races, so it was a perfect way to progress. The sport of Hard Enduro, which is what I was really interested in, was still in its infancy at the time, so the biggest part of my transition was actually waiting for the sport to grow. Not that I knew it would grow, so it still wasn't a career option! I just hoped it would. The main thing is that it had made me fall in love with riding motorbikes again and the fact that I was in my early-thirties, so not exactly a spring chicken, didn't even occur to me.

For anyone who doesn't know, Enduro races are run over extended cross-country and off-road courses and in terms of flow they are the antithesis of Trials. The difference between Enduro and Hard Enduro is simply down to the terrain which tends to be . . . well, harder. The clue's in the name. And it's harder not only on the riders but the equipment as well. Speaking of which, I forget which event it was but I once passed a pile of about a hundred knackered motorbikes.

Left Frying bacon in my burger van in 2009. I'll do anything for a few quid.

Below These two are the reason I get up in the morning. With Jack and Ellie at an event in 2009.

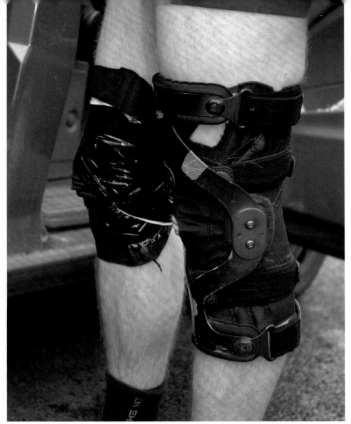

Left The price of success. Both my knees have given me problems over the years.

Below The calm before the storm. One minute to go before the 2015 Red Bull Megawatt.

Above On my way to my second win at the Erzberg, 2015.

Right Holding aloft my winner's trophy at the Erzberg in 2015. The smile says everything.

Left Me at the office during the 2015 Red Bull Sea to Sky. I can think of worse places to be.

Below left Winning Romaniacs in 2017. It's one of my favourite races and the people are tremendous.

Right At Hell's Gate – literally – in 2018. I had to settle for second this time around.

Below The Rockstar Husqvarna Team, 2019. From left to right, Billy Bolt, Aldredo Gomez and old man Jarvis.

Left Riding the Prologue at the 2019 Extreme Lagares in Portugal.

Below left With my friend and Rockstar Husqvarna team mate, Mario Gomez, after winning the 2019 Hixpania.

Right Conquering the Iron Giant, 2019.

Below Win number five at the Erzberg. I've got a lot of history with this race.

Negotiating a couple of rocks during the 2019 Hixpania. People keep asking me how long I can go on for, and to be honest I have no idea. Don't write me off just yet though.

A motorbike graveyard, if you like. If ever there was a picture that really sums up the harshness of this sport, that's got to be it.

By 2009 I was riding Hard Enduro full time but was earning even less money than I had been in Trials, if that were possible. Had I been more outgoing, then I dare say things might have been different. For a start I'd probably have had more sponsors, which would have been nice, but the ability to network just wasn't in me. Had I been able to, I'd have been pressing the flesh like nobody's business, but it just wasn't there.

By this time Sonya and I had also split up so it was a pretty bad time all round really, both emotionally and financially. Without wanting to go into too much detail, the split between Sonya and me had been acrimonious, and because of all the bad feeling I wasn't seeing the kids. Sometimes, when things aren't going well between two parents you have to live separate lives as it's not fair on the kids to see their parents fighting all the time. And so that's what I did. In hindsight I think both of us would have done things differently but at the time we were at each other's throats so it was for the best.

To supplement my ever-dwindling income I ended up buying a burger van – yes, seriously – and would tow it to and from the Enduro races to try and earn a few quid. My new girlfriend, Sandra, who I'm still with today, used to run it for me, and as soon as the race was over I'd have a wash, run over to the van and help out Sandra with the after-race rush. The look on the spectators' faces when they saw me flipping burgers was a picture. 'Weren't you just racing?' they'd all say. It was actually quite good for business.

By far the most surreal situation with regards to my career

in mobile catering was at one of the rounds of the 2009 British Trials championship which, just a year previously, I'd won for the last time. There were no Enduros that weekend, and one of the organisers of the round had asked me if I'd like to do the catering.

Some people might have been a bit embarrassed by this situation, but not me. I needed to earn some money in order to live and to carry on competing in Enduro and Hard Enduro, and at the end of the day, needs must. Some of the spectators thought it was hilarious seeing me flip burgers during the round, but others got a bit upset by it. A friend of mine called Ian Shankey came up afterwards and said he'd a tear in his eye watching me work in the van. He must have been thinking, *how the mighty have fallen*. Not too far, fortunately. I was simply starting afresh. Unlike the burgers. They were frozen.

I ended up keeping the burger van for about two or three years, and although I used it less and less once I'd found my feet in Hard Enduro, I kept it as a back-up. *Would you like onions with that, Madam?* See, I've still got it.

I actually remember the very first time I had a go on an Enduro bike, which are a lot heavier than Trials bikes and a lot more powerful. I asked a friend of mine who competed in the sport if I could borrow his bike one afternoon, and he was daft enough to say yes. It was a KTM 525, and I took it to a local motocross track. Psychologically, that was a bit of a faux pas as it was a whole new experience. Everything was completely alien to me, but at the time it hadn't clicked that the terrain I was riding on wasn't suitable for either the bike or the sport it was meant for. No wonder it felt wrong. It gets worse, though.

On the way back from this trip something must have hit the start button on the bike, and by the time I opened the doors to the van it was almost on fire. Needless to say, my mate wasn't very happy. He went mental.

The ideal bike for Hard Enduro is a 250 or 300cc two-stroke. A four-stroke's OK, but they're a bit too heavy for Hard Enduro.

What first attracted me to Enduro, and subsequently Hard Enduro, was actually just the concept of riding your bike quickly off-road, à la Scott Trial or the Scottish Six Days, but without the observed sections. It's such a simple concept compared to Trials. I first heard about the sport somewhere donkey's years ago and I remember thinking, *God, that sounds brilliant!* It was never on TV, though, so, as daft as it may sound, the first time I actually got a taste of the Enduro was when I first entered a race. That would have been some time in 2006.

The event in question was a local Enduro lasting two and a half hours, and the thing I remember most about it is how physically demanding it was. I was knackered afterwards! What I also realised was how natural it felt and how easy it was for me to be immediately competitive. In that particular race, of course. I realised that on anything technical, like a log, I was instantly faster, and safer, than most of the other riders. Sure, I was competing against amateurs, but there were still a handful of riders who could beat me on the fast going. Things would get tougher as I moved up, but I enjoyed every minute of that first race. It was a revelation.

This may sound a bit conceited, but the truth is that in that first race I was better than the majority of the other riders – and I'd never even tried it before. It was a surprise really and I remember thinking to myself, *Why is everybody else so rubbish?* I promise you, that's just the professional sportsperson talking, and as opposed to me simply running the other riders down I was sensing an opportunity.

If you talk to people who haven't done Enduro before but have seen a race, they assume that everyone's riding flat out, but that isn't the case. Or at least it isn't always the case. People are simply riding to the best of their ability, whether that be fast, very fast or not very fast at all. Everyone's experience is different. I know that sounds obvious, but some people think we're all going through the same motions. We're not, believe me, and it really is as mad as it looks. There's an awful lot of technique, though, which isn't always appreciated. You can't just take your brains out and twist the throttle.

Certain parts of Enduro and Hard Enduro can be related directly to Trials, such as riding over rocks and logs. That technique is almost identical in both sports, in terms of approach and execution. So Trials riders will have an advantage over people who are starting from scratch or who are coming in from another motorcycle sport such as motocross. What I found difficult, though, and what didn't come quite as naturally to me, were things like riding flat corners and riding through sand. Things like that had to be worked on, and especially in a competitive environment, although it didn't take me long to catch on. I'll never be the fastest on those conditions but I can do it well enough.

When I became established in Hard Enduro, which I suppose would have been in 2009, it was suggested to me by a journalist that, given how extreme Trials can be with regards to the terrain – as in, it's like rock-climbing on a bike – I was taking a step down going to Hard Enduro. I kind of knew what he was getting at (he considered Trials to be more skilful), but despite some similarities, Trials and Hard Enduro are massively different, so you can't really compare the two. I suppose nobdy knew back then how massive Hard Enduro would become (even me).

That said, the transition from Trials to Enduro or Hard Enduro is usually quite smooth, and it's no coincidence that so many Trials riders make the switch. I think we all have an issue with the speed at first, but learning to adapt your skills should see you through. Trials gives you everything you need to succeed in the two sports: clutch control, throttle control, finding grip, looking for lines. It's all there if you've come from Trials. As I just said, a lot of riders are crossing over these days. Apart from me you've got the Hemingway brothers, who compete at both, but even the biggest Hard Enduro stars such as Billy Bolt, Taddy Błażusiak, Alfredo Gómez and Jonny Walker cut their teeth in Trials. In fact, Alfredo was the junior world Trials champion back in 2011.

I think balance also has a lot to do with it – taking on the rocks and the logs. It's a lot harder coming from motocross, as you don't have the clutch control, and you don't necessarily know how to tackle obstacles. Another reason why British riders tend to make the transition easily is the weather factor. We're all used to riding in the cold and wet, so if that's what we're facing, and it often is with Hard Enduro, then so be it. Chuck a bit of sun our way, however, which you get with quite a lot of the big races such as Roof of Africa, and we're all over it like a rash.

What's unique about Trials is that the vast majority of

spectators will have ridden to a decent level. As one of the cheapest forms of motorsport, it's always been more about participation than aspiration and the vast majority of spectators attending a Trial will have ridden from a young age. So rather than just having an opinion based on what they've seen or read, it will be based on what they've experienced, and there aren't many sports that can make that claim, including Hard Enduro. It's one of the reasons there's such a family atmosphere in Trials, and although I've often appreciated it from afar, as I was too shy to mingle with other people, I have still appreciated it.

The rivalries are also quite friendly in Trials, and I suppose one of the reasons for that is because you're never actually racing against each other at the same time. It's obviously very different with things like motocross (and to a lesser extent Hard Enduro). Some of the stories I've heard about motocross would make your teeth itch. Quite a few of those boys can't stand each other, and because there's a lot of contact, or at least there can be a lot of contact, the arguments will often spill over onto the track. In fact, I dare say that the majority of them start on the track.

In my early days in Enduro and Hard Enduro I still rode for Sherco, but instead of having a contract or receiving a wage they just paid my expenses. It sounds like I'm complaining here, but I'm not. Sherco had just brought out their new Enduro bike – their first – and because I hadn't had much success in the sport, it was actually a good deal. Also, Hard Enduro was still very young at the time and comparing the races then to the races today – certainly in terms of prize money and exposure – is like comparing chalk and cheese.

It was early days for everybody, and even the big races were tiny in comparison to now.

My first big win in Hard Enduro had come the year before this in 2008 when I won the Red Bull Romaniacs in Romania. That was, I suppose, the announcement that I'd arrived on the Hard Enduro scene, and it made the organisers, the spectators and the manufacturers sit up and take notice. In fact, the only person who didn't really notice was me. In terms of its prestige I came away from Romaniacs none the wiser, and it was only when I competed at the 2008 Trials des Nations, which I did for the last time, that I started to get an idea. Somebody came up to me and started telling me what a big achievement it was to win Romaniacs. The thing is – and some of you will think I'm pulling a fast one here – the only thing I found difficult about that race was the navigation, and if I had to choose one word to describe the experience, I'd probably say 'enjoyable'. It was fun. Some of the terrain was a bit challenging, but that just kept me interested. The scenery was also breathtaking and the people were great, so all in all it was a good four days. That was about it, though. It takes a lot to get me animated!

The point this bloke at the Trials des Nations kept on making was that a Trials rider who'd done a couple of local Enduros should not be able to enter the Romaniacs and win it first time around on a 250cc four-stroke, but because I'd found it so easy that particular fact was lost on me. Once again, I was slow on the uptake. Speaking of which.

I made the massive mistake of camping at the Erzberg in 2009, and it's something I still kick myself about. I'll be introducing the Erzberg properly a bit later on, as it's safe to say I've had one or two 'incidents' there over the years, not to mention one or two wins. For those of you who've never been, it's basically party central in the camping area, and the night before the race the noise was just incredible. Everybody was on the piss, everybody was playing loud music and everybody was having a great time – except me. As well as feeling like a tit for having put myself in that situation, I was getting more and more frustrated and tired. I was also going to be starting the race from the third row after my gear lever came loose in the prologue and that was also playing on my mind. In the end I went to see the loudest perpetrators and asked them if they'd mind turning it down a bit.

'Graham Jarvis, whoooo!' said the first perpetrator, who was at least twelve sheets to the wind.

'Yes, that's right.'

'What the bloody hell are you doing here? You should be in a hotel somewhere getting some sleep.'

No shit, Sherlock!

'I'm camping,' I mumbled.

'You're what?'

'I'm camping.'

'What, here?'

'Yes, here!'

I was starting to get pissed off now.

'Hey, look everyone,' shouted my drunken friend. 'It's Graham Jarvis. He's camping!'

What a bloody cock-up.

I ended up signing autographs and having my photograph taken with just about everybody there, and I can't remember what time I got to sleep – 3 or 4 a.m., maybe?

You're often running on adrenalin on race day, but a few hours' sleep certainly doesn't do you any harm. In fact, it's essential at the big races and the multi-day events.

As I said, because of the gear lever fiasco I ended up having a shit run in the prologue. I was also riding the four-stroke, so all things considered – wrong bike, no sleep, third row – I didn't fancy my chances much. Luckily, I managed to get the holeshot on my row but I still had another hundred riders to pass from rows one and two. That's essential at the Erzberg, as the start is usually chaos. Get away quickly and you stand a good chance of getting out of the quarry where it starts. Get away slowly and your chances shrink to almost zero. In this case, getting out of the quarry with the leaders was totally against the form books, as it's safe to say that starts are not my speciality. To be the first out from the third row was a bonus but the quarry was already full of bikes flying in all directions and somehow I didn't get hit by one. I'd never seen anything as chaotic in my entire life, but the excitement, and the fact that it was every man for himself, made it somehow addictive. I remember passing people and thinking, *What the bloody hell's going on?!* I ended up passing ninety-nine of those other riders to finish second behind Taddy Błażusiak.

One of the best things about Hard Enduro is that each race is a real adventure, and you have to use every ounce of ingenuity you have. It's like *Raiders of the Lost Ark* on motorbikes. For example, I remember breaking down during Romaniacs one year, and I ended up mending the bike with a stick. I was still riding a four-stroke, so it would have been the early days, and towards the end of the last day the bike started running badly. The spark plug cap had melted, so after pushing what was left of it in with a stick, I tried nursing the bike back. In the end I dropped short of the finish by about an hour and because there was nobody else around and no telephone signal I had to go into survival mode. An hour might not sound like much, but you can travel a long way on a bike in that time, and up in the mountains, which is where a lot of Romaniacs takes place, things can get quite wild. I'd heard stories about people being out all night during the race and because I had no idea how long I was going to be there I decided to build a shelter and then light a fire. I'd watched Bear Grylls on television so I thought I'd give it a go. In the end the shelter wasn't too much of a problem, but I couldn't find any dry wood, although I did have a lighter on me. As the light began to fade and the temperature dropped I started to panic. In a fit of desperation I tried to burn the air filter from the bike but it burst into flames and then quickly died. After four very cold hours I was finally located, by which time I was a shivering wreck. Because of how close I'd got to the finish I only received a two-hour penalty, and because of the gap I'd created during the previous three days I still ended up finishing second. How mad is that?

More often than not I used to drive myself, and my bike, to and from the Hard Enduro races in those early days. In that respect it was like my early days in Trials. It was just me and the open road. I should point out that I didn't remain unsupported for long, as after a while Sherco arranged for the importers in whatever country I was competing in to look after me once I'd arrived. It was never an especially professional set-up, but it was better than nothing. There'd be a van, a lot of mess, a gazebo, an importer and me. Welcome to team Jarvis!

These days I fly to races, thank God, and am met by a professional team that includes my long-time mechanic and chief piss-taker, Damien Butler – Damo.

The only specific regret I have about my transition from Trials to Hard Enduro also happened in 2007, and as well as exemplifying my assertion that I'm a bit of a late starter, it could have changed everything, as it would have catapulted me to the top of the sport. I had a chance to ride at the Erzberg that year, but it clashed with a round of the British Trials championship and although I was desperate to go I decided to honour my contract with Malcolm. Even then the Erzberg was a big event, and that year it was being sponsored by KTM. Taddy BłaÐusiak, who was my long-time rival at the Erzberg, ended up getting a factory ride with KTM after competing in and subsequently winning that particular race, and he went on to dominate Hard Enduro for the next few years. Or at least until I took over the mantle.

I know regrets aren't healthy, but looking back I should have been selfish and chosen the bloody Erzberg. Then again, if I had gone over there and been offered a contract with KTM I might have peaked in my very early forties! Heaven forbid. I'll let you know when I do peak.

The only other Brits I remember being on the Hard Enduro scene at the time were Paul Bolton, who's done really well, Julian Stevens, who is also an excellent mechanic, and the celebrated Enduro rider David Knight, or Knighter as he's known. By then Knighter was already a three-time world Enduro champion and had also won the Erzberg twice, so he wasn't a bad lad to have around. Then again, neither was Paul or Julian.

I remember arriving at the Erzberg for the first time and Julian was putting a disc protector on Knighter's bike. 'Do I need one of them?' I asked. Julian just looked at me as if I was a lunatic. 'Of course you bloody do,' he said finally. 'You do know what you're doing, don't you, Graham?' To be honest, I wasn't sure, and to an onlooker it might have seemed like I'd turned up to the wrong event. *Sorry, mate. Trials are that way.* I'd only been competing in the sport for a few months, it had only been occasionally, so to all intents and purposes I was still a bungling amateur.

I remember going to a local Enduro meeting once and at some point during the day somebody started talking to me about Enduro tyres and motocross tyres. 'Is there a difference?' I asked them. Once again, I was stared at as though I was an alien, but the truth is I didn't know the answer. 'Motocross tyres are thicker than Enduro tyres and are FIM-approved', said my knowledgeable tutor. 'Really,' I said, sounding interested. It was news to me! To paraphrase a popular saying, in my early days in Enduro and Hard Enduro I had some of the gear, but virtually no idea!

There was nothing normal about this situation. I was thirty-one years of age and had just started competing in one of the most dangerous and physically demanding motorsports out there. Also – this was only in the early days – I'd sometimes see a rider halfway through a race who I recognised, and I'd think to myself, *Wow, it's him!* The first time this happened was at the Erzberg, I think. Or was it Hell's Gate? Anyway, the rider in question was the Dakar Rally legend, Cyril Despres. I remember catching him during the race before having a bit of a battle with him and all I could think was, *Bloody hell, it's Cyril Despres!* It was a hell of a lot different to meeting Steve Saunders in a television studio or seeing Jordi Tarrés in his motorhome. It was more than just star spotting. I was racing against legends.

People sometimes ask me what kind of condition I was in physically when I left Trials and they're often left wondering how a decrepit old git like me could possibly compete in a sport as demanding and as intense as Hard Enduro. Well, apart from being superhuman, I've always looked after myself and falling off motorcycles occasionally notwithstanding, I've never abused my body – apart from a few drunken nights. If that isn't a good enough explanation, I'd have to say luck!

I read an interview with Malcolm the other day by Sean Lawless and when they got on to the subject of me, Malcolm said, 'He was semi-knackered when he left us. He had two knackered knees and a knackered back. I think everything he's done now he learned from the Scott Trial.'

That last bit is obviously true but then so is the first bit. In order to fully appreciate just how demanding Hard Enduro is you have to experience it firsthand, and I wouldn't wish that on anybody who wasn't physically fit. Staying on top of aches and pains is a constant battle but I've learnt to manage them with stretches and strengthening. I have good days and bad days (doesn't everybody?), but it's not getting any easier.

Things were a bit of a struggle in 2009 as Sherco couldn't offer me any real support at races so basically I was a privateer. Then, at the end of 2009 I was approached by the Goldentyre-backed Flite team, which was based in Italy. They'd been impressed by my performances so far in Hard Enduro and were keen to do a deal. After explaining my current arrangement they made an agreement with Sherco to support me at races, which was obviously the missing piece of the jigsaw. For the first time in my life I didn't have to worry about anything other than riding my bike and that was both empowering and liberating. From now on I would fly to the races instead of driving and would literally just turn up, get on the bike and ride. At last!

By this time Hard Enduro had probably taken over Enduro in terms of popularity, as races like the Erzberg, Hell's Gate and Romaniacs were growing rapidly and Enduro didn't really have an equivalent. As soon as I signed for Flite I knew I'd done the right thing. They too could see the potential of Hard Enduro, and they were both experienced and professional, which was exactly what I needed.

Hell's Gate was the first big race of 2010 and at the time it was by far the biggest race in Italy, so it was obviously important to the team. Goldentyre had developed a soft tyre that I'd be using, and they were working hard to improve it. There were three guys in the Flite team and they were all there just for me. It was a dream! The only downside to the new arrangement was the Sherco, which was a four-stroke and a bit unreliable.

Like the others, Hell's Gate, despite the scary name, didn't mean much to me back then. The race was first introduced in 2006 by the Italian Enduro legend Fabio Fasola, and it immediately became like a magnet for the world's best off-road motorcyclists. It takes place on a privately owned mountain called Il Ciocco, which is in Tuscany, and the paddock is located about a ten-minute drive into the range where the mountain's situated. There's a hotel close by, so it's not too inaccessible, and while it's not the biggest race on the calendar anymore, it's particularly difficult to ride and the atmosphere is electric – especially right at the end.

After a five-hour qualifier race in the morning, the

remaining 30 riders will move on to compete in the main event which takes place in the afternoon and evening. It takes place on an 11-mile course over steep hills and rocky climbs and during the break headlights will be fitted to the bikes in preparation for the dark. Suffice to say that it can, and has, produced some of the most exciting finishes you'll ever see in Hard Enduro.

When I first raced there, I had to hitch a lift over for both me and my bike, and nobody gave me a chance on the 450cc. To be honest, I don't remember a great deal about the race, save for the fact that it was hard and that some of it took place in the dark. The other thing I remember, apart from it being the longest day I'd ever had on a motorbike, is that I finished fourth overall, and, because of the bike I was riding, it was probably another occasion that made a few people sit up and take notice of what I was potentially capable of in the sport.

In 2010, from the 30 of the 103 riders who went through from the four laps of qualifying in the morning, only two riders finished the final four laps in the afternoon. I'll come on to who they were in a second. The reason I want to concentrate on this particular race is that it reignited an old rivalry – one that, until recently, I'd considered to be over. It came about because of the emergence onto the Hard Enduro scene of a certain Dougie Lampkin.

I have massive respect for Dougie. We may not be best pals, but we've spent a lot of time together over the years. When Dougie turns up at an event you know he's not there to make up the numbers and you're not just competing against him. You're competing against the Lampkin dynasty. When I heard he was going to be competing in a few Hard Enduro races I genuinely remember saying to myself something along the lines of, *Oh Christ, not him again. Not Lampkin!* Dougie had been my nemesis all throughout my adult Trials career and the thought of him turning up and reprising his role in Hard Enduro was almost too much to bear. Just piss off and leave me alone, Dougie, please!

He might have competed in a few smaller races prior to Hell's Gate in 2010, but if he had, they'd passed me by, and this is the first one I can remember. In fact, I remember it all too well! How many Trials world championships had he won again? Sixty-four? In a newish sport that I was on the verge of dominating, he really was the last thing I needed.

I think Taddy was the initial leader on those final four laps but I caught him up, and he ended up crashing heavily after hitting some ice on one of the highest sections of the track. I'm pretty sure he broke his front brake. He was looking really good at the time, so he must have been gutted. I certainly wasn't!

After Taddy dropped out, I took the lead, and by lap three there was just me, Dougie and Andreas Lettenbichler left in the race. At Hell's Gate, riders who are more than forty minutes behind the leader at any given checkpoint are immediately pulled out of the race, and unfortunately for Andreas he was soon one of them. That just left me and Dougie.

Dougie was about seven minutes behind me when Andreas dropped out, so although he wasn't going to be removed at a checkpoint, barring a disaster I knew I would be standing in the middle of the podium at the end of the race with Dougie to my left. For me to beat Dougie for a change, and in a sport I'd come to love and felt comfortable in – it was truly the stuff that dreams were made of.

Towards the end of Hell's Gate, you do about an hour in the dark, and literally a few minutes after darkness had descended I crashed and smashed my headlight. I couldn't believe it! I was making mistakes now and fatigue was setting in. Just riding flat ground was becoming a challenge. Somehow I managed to get myself to the final hill, which is called Hell's Peak, but because I couldn't see where I was going I hit it badly. Well, that's my excuse. Had I hit Hell's Peak like I usually did, I'd have been home and dry. After cocking it up, I was anything but. It was a bad attempt, but I was far enough up the peak to get hooked onto a rope that had been lowered down by the fans. It doesn't happen anymore, but because of the steepness of the peak the Italian fans used to help riders by lowering down a huge rope and then pulling them up. It was one of Italian Hard Enduro's most glorious traditions and it made the sport unique.

Once me and my bike were hooked onto the rope, a long line of fans started pulling supposedly for all they were worth. Slowly but surely, me and my bike started crawling up the peak but at the rate we were moving it was going to be a good three or four minutes before I reached the top. About a minute later, I suddenly heard the unmistakable sound of an approaching Lampkin. Bugger! The Italians were lapping this up – there were at least two thousand Hard Enduro fanatics at the top of Hell's Peak and Dougie was riding a Beta, which is an Italian manufacturer – as Dougie, who had the famous Lampkin chin in full grimace, flew past me and the fans swiftly pulled him up. I remember finally dragging myself over the brow of the peak and the first thing I saw was Dougie celebrating with his mechanic and a few thousand excitable Italians. It was a pretty demoralising sight to be honest, and it evoked all kinds of horrible memories.

One of the reasons I'd been so intent on winning the race is because the first prize was a 450cc KTM worth about £6,000. I was skint at the time and it would have seen me through the next few months. Instead, I got a trophy. Despite the disappointment, this was actually a turning point as I had no intention of leaving Hard Enduro and I did not want history to repeat itself again.

While steadily growing in popularity, Hard Enduro was still a bit of an unknown quantity, and I don't think anybody really knew how to commercialise it. None of the factories were throwing any money at it and because it hadn't found its feet on YouTube yet, or even Facebook, nobody was interested. At least commercially. It wouldn't take long to change, but when I first started competing in Hard Enduro I was constantly skint and became an expert in getting by on bugger all. For example, on a Thursday I might get on a flight to a race and would be met at the airport by the team. They'd put me up in a nice hotel and on race day I'd be picked up and driven to its location. After the race, if I won, I'd be handed a bottle of champagne on the podium and after spraying some of the spectators and fellow riders I'd go and do some interviews. After that I'd travel home victorious, full of the joys of life, and then happily get into bed. The following morning I'd get up, get in the van, and go and practise somewhere. I didn't have much in the way of expenses, so once I'd paid the kids' maintenance money, all I had to think about was food and fuel. Clothes-wise, I've always tended to go for teamwear, as it's usually free, so my expenditure in that department was next to nothing. It still is. I was also living with Sandra by then, and because she already had her own house I was cheaper to run than most motorbikes.

I'd first met Sandra in 2006 at a KTM dealership in Ripon called Eurotek, which is where she used to work. I asked her for the bit of wire that connects your back brake to your sump shield. 'You mean a brake snake?' she said. I remember thinking, *she knows her stuff!*

Since splitting up with Sonya, I'd become a bit of a recluse and had only recently started going out again. A New Zealander called Phil who worked for Malcolm had come to lodge with me for a bit, and because he liked a drink I started tagging along. This was a new experience for me, as I'd never really gone out drinking before. I'd been out a few times with Rob and Colin, but that was when I was much younger.

Although I fancied her, I was too shy to speak to Sandra about anything other than bike parts, so in the end a mutual friend of ours called Ian told her to take me out on the lash one night. It wasn't a date, as such. In fact, Sandra was supposed to be taking me out on the pull. Not an easy task.

When Sandra arrived at the place we were meeting, I was clutching a pint of tap water. I still hadn't found my drinking boots, despite living with a New Zealander, and only tended to drink when there was a chance of some action. Then I'd have a couple, just to give me some Dutch courage! Sandra was horrified when she saw the water and quickly ordered some two-for-one cocktails. We chatted about everything except biker and I learnt to laugh again, before dancing the night away in a very cheesy nightclub called Flares. Apparently I did a very good line in Mr Bean dancing that night!

Sandra's not a particular fan of Enduro, which is good, so

we were able to talk about other things. I'm not saying I had a one-track mind or anything, but that was probably the first time I'd ever gone a whole evening without talking shop.

Signing for Flite was the big turning point for me and everything started to click. Goldentyre had just brought out some revolutionary soft tyres for Hard Enduro which nobody else had, so for the first time in my life I had the upper hand. Well, almost. The only thing hindering us now was the bike and in the end we had to sever ties with Sherco and look for something else. As you can imagine, this was an incredibly difficult decision as Marc Tessier had supported me since 1994 and he and his staff had basically become my French family.

Over the years I'd always put loyalty before anything else and back in 2001 this had been put to the ultimate test when, completely out of the blue, I received an approach from Gas Gas. I was in the top five in the world at the time but the loyalty I felt towards Malcolm and Rhoda was at its height. I was also living with their daughter at the time, so it felt wrong. When I told Malcolm I'd turned them down he got really upset and insisted that I go and see them. I still turned them down, and in hindsight I wish I hadn't as they might well have been the difference between me finishing fourth in the world and finishing first. I couldn't let that happen again so with a heavy heart we moved from Sherco and did a deal with the Husaberg factory who had just released a 300cc 2-Stroke. The bike was basically a re-badged KTM as they owned Husaberg and although I wasn't going to be a full factory rider the bike was amazing, so I didn't care.

Previously, the only factory rider in Hard Enduro had been Taddy, and although I'd won the odd race, he was seen as being the man to beat. He was the Dougie Lampkin of Hard Enduro, if you like. Once I was up to speed and properly supported, it was game on, and I didn't waste any time winning races. As well as looking after me at races, Flite also paid for me to practise at their base in Italy. The boss of the team, Marco Caribotti, who at one time rode motocross, also used to come riding with me, as did his right hand man, Christian.

By the time I left Sherco I felt almost as much loyalty to Marc as I did to Malcolm and Rhoda. He used to fill in as minder for me when Malcolm couldn't make it, and at every single world round I ever won Marc had tears in his eyes. You can't put a price on good people, and I had three of the best.

Before I decided to leave, I went to see Malcolm and Rhoda to ask their advice. I told them that I'd had an offer, but I was worried about being disloyal to them and Sherco.

'This time you've got to go,' said Malcolm, so that's exactly what I did. My relationship with Sherco had lasted over ten years and my relationship with Malcolm and Rhoda almost double that, but like all good things it eventually had to come to an end. There were no hard feelings between Malcolm, Rhoda and me, and instead of lamenting what might have been had I moved over to Hard Enduro sooner, we concentrated on what we'd achieved in Trials, which was massive.

Although we didn't fall out as such, Marc found it difficult to speak to me for a while after I left, which was an awful situation to be in. I thought he hated me, but according to Malcolm and Rhoda he simply needed time to come to terms with my decision. Marc's a very emotional man, and the tears he'd shed at the world rounds I'd won had been real. I'm happy to report that he and I are talking again now, and given what I've gone on to achieve I think he understands why I made the choice I did.

As far as I was concerned, I had found something I was good at that didn't play havoc with my nerves, and if I hadn't gone with Husaberg, I'd have been doing it so as not to upset Marc. Was that a good enough reason not to further my career and give myself a chance of earning a few quid and being the best in my field? As much as I like and respect Marc – and I do – I'm afraid it wasn't, and I had no choice but to walk away. Also, the bike Sherco were supplying me with was not going to give me the chance to win consistently, so that too forced my hand.

Funnily enough, Sherco have gone on to become one of the most successful manufacturers in Hard Enduro and although their riders are obviously competitors of mine, I don't be-grudge them the odd win!

The following year I have to admit that Hell's Gate bought a wave of fear. That KTM was still lingering in my mind, as was Dougie. He'd been doing quite well since the last Hell's Gate, and he'd won a couple of other events.

By the time I reached Italy my mood had changed a bit. I was being tipped to do the grand slam that year, and having already won the Tough One it was on. Granted, there were still five more races to win, but I had a good feeling about it, and a lot of people were backing me.

The organisers had made it as tough as ever. The first ses-sion would include forty minutes of special test racing, which is a time-card event where you have to go flat out for five or ten minutes during a lap. The afternoon session would consist of six laps, with each taking roughly an hour. It was obviously going to be tough.

As expected, the morning session was crippling, but after coming out on top I started the main event feeling fresh and sitting on pole position. The afternoon session started like a road race with a grid. True to form, I didn't start especially strongly and, after failing to fire my bike into life as the flag dropped, I was beaten to the holeshot by my fellow Husaberg rider, Xavier Galindo. Despite that I soon managed to get past Xavier, and by the time I reached the first major spectator point I had a three-minute lead. I remember feeling pretty good at this point, and to be honest I'd forgotten about Dougie. All I could think about was the grand slam.

As my lead continued to grow, the organisers kept pulling riders out of the race, and by the fourth lap my lead was so long that the organisers decided that they'd have to cut it short. As opposed to it being six laps, they'd stop the race after four. About half an hour later, I arrived at the foot of Hell's Peak, tired and sore, but with a massive lead and fully working lights! There must have been at least two thousand people scattered across that Italian hillside. I was tired but I made sure of it this time and within seconds of me coming to a halt about fifty people ran over and started pulling my bike up with me. It was an incredible moment, as it was going to be my first ever win at Hell's Gate, which they all seemed to realise. The peak is near vertical, by the way, so after six hours you need all the help you can get.

By the time I got over the line – I was virtually carried over – my lead was still just under twenty-five minutes, and

I'd eliminated every rider, except . . . Dougie Lampkin. That was a really good day's work, and it's one of the sweetest wins I've ever had.

After that it went mercifully quiet on the Dougie front and although he competed a few more times I usually managed to beat him. In 2012, however, he made his presence felt one last time. The details of this particular race, or at least the end of it, are in the Erzberg section, which is coming up, but in short, after crossing the finish line first, I was then disqualified and as a consequence of this Dougie, who had been in third, moved up a position on the podium. I remember pulling away from him at Carl's Diner, which is the most gruelling section of the Erzberg, and I remember thinking to myself, Who's the boss now, sorry, Dougie. Then, literally a few seconds after finishing first, I get disqualified! I was mortified at the time and I don't mind admitting that when Dougie gave up competing in Hard Enduro it was a big relief.

Being magnanimous for a second, had Dougie had the hunger and desire he could well have become a force in the sport, and he would obviously have done its profile no harm whatsoever. In fact, whenever Dougie did compete in a Hard Enduro race he was a big draw for both the press and spectators alike, and had he competed regularly he would have raised everybody's game. I obviously can't speak for him, but it is possible that because he'd been so successful in Trials he didn't have the motivation to start again. Twelve world championships and seven or eight years at the top would probably have seen to that. I, on the other hand, was the hungry fighter and experiencing more success than I'd ever had in Trials, so for me it was a no-brainer. I also preferred

Hard Enduro as a sport (and still do), whereas I doubt that would be the case for Dougie. He's every inch a Trials man, and given his family history it would be hard to imagine him championing something else.

Before we leave Hell's Gate, there a quick story I've just remembered.

There's a part of Hell's Gate called Cascarta, which is Italian for waterfall, and one year as I was riding down it a rope got caught in my back wheel. I think they'd been using them to walk bikes down or something, but I hadn't seen it. It obviously stopped me dead, and I went flying over the handlebars and down into the water. It's on YouTube, and when I fall all you can hear are Italians shouting, 'Mamma Mia!'.

For the next two years I won everything in sight and was just about unstoppable. I'd experienced a version of this when I was in Trials, but only as a schoolboy. I remember turning up to Trials, wiping the floor with everybody, and then walking away thinking, *What happened there?* It was a feeling of invincibility because I always had the deep desire to win, which I realise now not everyone has. If anything, I found winning slightly embarrassing and didn't understand why I kept on beating everybody and why it felt so easy. I was only competing against my age group and lads from the UK, of course, and if I had to offer younger riders any advice at all it would be that winning championships as a youth doesn't guarantee you success as an adult. So instead of getting carried away, just try and enjoy it.

Not being able to repeat that in adulthood had sat heavily on my shoulders and despite my successes I was always going to be remembered – in Trials, at least – as the lad from Kent who didn't quite fulfil his potential. People would probably mention the Scott Trials and the British championships, but the crux of the conversations would always be what hadn't happened and what could have.

Football is full of people like that – players who are compared to past legends or are labelled as being the next big thing – and it's usually a kiss of death. Unless they go on to achieve greatness, they too will forever be remembered as a player who, ultimately, failed.

By becoming a success in my mid-thirties, and in a sport that was relatively new, meant that I wasn't going to be compared to anybody, and I was too old to be thought of as somebody who was merely showing potential. This was it. This was Graham Jarvis, the Hard Enduro rider.

Please don't think I'm being conceited here. I had to go through a lot to get to this position, and the fact that I actually made it, and at the grand old age of thirty-five, is a great source of pride to me. And relief! It just goes to show though that anything can happen. Even to old people.

10

At the same time that I started to win races, I also noticed the effect social media was having on the sport. Facebook especially was becoming absolutely massive at that time, and the riders and race organisers were posting photos and videos like there was no tomorrow. Because Hard Enduros often take place in extreme locations, getting to them isn't always easy, and because what we do is considered to be quite dangerous – not to mention exciting at times – we were able to give fans a sense of the events via social media. It was something new at the time, and people couldn't get enough of it. Hard Enduro often mixes spectacular scenery with agony, torment, anguish and speed, so it's pretty unique in that respect.

I actually remember the first time I was filmed by somebody at a race. Or at least with my knowledge. This bloke was holding a mobile phone as if taking a picture, and as I passed him he said, 'I'm filming this.' The following day, he sent it to me on my Facebook and within just a few hours of me posting it, it had been viewed and shared tens of thousands of times. I don't think I'd had my page up long, and to be honest I hadn't been taking it all that seriously. I thought

Facebook was for talking to people so I obviously didn't need it. I had no idea how important it was going to be. Not just to me, but to the growth of our sport. After that, whether I was training or taking part in a race, I'd always make sure that whoever was with me would have a camera pointing in my direction. The first person to do this was Christian, Marco's right-hand man. From the team's point of view – as well as the sponsors' – this was also a game changer, as instead of the sponsors' logos being seen by a few thousand people in person or in a magazine they were suddenly being seen by – at the time – tens or even hundreds of thousands of people online. Everything started to change.

Then, in 2011, a company called Adventure Spec called me up and said they'd like to sponsor me. As ridiculous as this may sound, that was the first time a company had ever called me up to ask if they could sponsor me. I couldn't believe it! To find out what I was worth they'd been in touch with Cyril Despres' manager and had arrived at the figure of £10,000.

'What do I have to do for that'? I asked suspiciously.

'Well,' they said, 'you'll have to do some videos for us. You know, corporate stuff.'

'Yeah, I can do that.'

'And you'll have to wear some clothing.'

I tried playing it cool by saying I'd think about it but in truth I was in disbelief and couldn't stop smiling!

They must have thought they were dealing with a child! Then again, the last direct sponsorship I'd done was for Big Bertha and before that it had been a jacket, so in a way they were. It was great, though. Ten grand!

I suppose this was when I realised that I might be able to do more than just scrape by in Hard Enduro, providing I carried on winning, of course, which I was. And providing I updated my social media regularly, which I did.

It was actually the guys at Adventure Spec who suggested we start taking the video thing more seriously, and they offered to pay for somebody to produce some films for me as long as they could put them on their YouTube channel. Given the reaction to the ones Christian had filmed on his phone, this was obviously a good idea, so that's exactly what we did. The potential was clearly massive, and we wanted to be at the forefront.

In addition to growing my own profile and giving exposure to the team and sponsors, producing videos would present the sport in a more professional light, which was also very important at that time. There were parts of the sport that were run quite professionally and parts of it that weren't – but that was only because it was growing. We were just catching up. What was important at the time was to make the public face of Hard Enduro, which was basically all social media, as polished, impressive and attractive to fans and potential fans as was humanly possible, and Adventure Spec seemed to have the answer.

The cameraman we used, although he would call himself a film-maker, was Mikey Lonsdale – a complete and utter nutcase who's good at coming up with ideas and knows how to hold a camera. The first one we did was with the comedian Ross Noble. Some of you will probably already know this, but Ross is a Trials and Hard Enduro fanatic, and as well as completing the Scottish Six Days Trial, which was the subject of a three-part series he did for the TV channel Dave entitled *Off Road*, he also finished Romaniacs in 2011.

Anyway, the idea was that I would join Ross and a few

other riders at the Toro Trail, which is an Enduro tour centre in Malaga. As well as all of us riding together, Ross and I would do some interviews about life, Hard Enduro and everything else. Despite us having fun, Ross wasn't happy with the final product, and unfortunately that was my fault as my non-stop witty banter just wasn't cutting the mustard and he felt the interview sections were lacking a bit, surprise surprise. Subsequently, instead of sticking with the original idea our intrepid cameraman – sorry, film-maker – put together a montage of the best bits of me on a bike. The residential part of Toro Trial is quite an impressive set-up, and they had me riding around the swimming pool and what have you, doing tricks and things and jumping over tables. The final shot is of me in a hot tub wearing just my helmet and the entire thing lasts just over four minutes.

The video was made in March 2012, and to date it's been watched almost 12 million times, and that's just on YouTube. It was probably the first of its kind with regards to Hard Enduro and people still come up to me today and tell me that it was what inspired them to take up the sport. Apart from winning a race, I think I get more gratification from that than anything else I do when it comes to bikes. Watching the sport grow has been incredible, and it's a pleasure being part of it. In fact, it's probably the only thing I've ever done where I could be described as being a pioneer, because with most things, as you well know, I was normally playing catch-up.

After that we made a film about me taking part in a local Trial, and that one also went viral. I think Mikey came up with the name G-Force Jarvis around this time, and the title of the film, which is on YouTube, is *The Adventures of G-Force Jarvis – Going Back to his Roots*. Incidentally, the name G-Force Jarvis was never meant to become a professional nickname or anything. We weren't creating a brand. It was just something Mikey started calling me and after a while it stuck. It's better than Grimbo, I suppose!

I'd been invited to take part in this local Trial just for a bit of fun, and Mikey thought it would be a good idea to make a film out of it. I was riding my Enduro bike and the storyline – yes, we actually had one for this film – was that I'd overindulged at Christmas and needed to get on my bike in order to lose a few pounds. It was all very tongue in cheek, and everybody there got into the spirit of things. That film was actually quite important, as a lot of people who followed me in foreign countries had had no idea about my background in Trials, so it made people ask questions. That one also got well over a million views, and it's one of my favourites.

Of all the videos I've either filmed or have been involved in there's one that, from an audience point of view, is head and shoulders above the rest. It was filmed in Leeds at an indoor skate park called The Works and is basically just me riding my bike around and doing a few tricks. It might be a simple concept, but it obviously hadn't been done before, and because we were the first to do it, the film, which is just seven minutes long, has gone on to receive over 20 million views. Shorter videos seem to work for some reason. In 2017 I put some highlights up of the season just gone which was just over a minute long and within a few weeks it had been viewed over 4 million times!

What's taken all this to another level are the helmet cams. Once again I was one of the first to use one, and although they'd been around a while the majority of riders weren't keen on them. I think this is one of the reasons I've got so many followers on social media – that and the fact that I win the odd race, I suppose. The reason the other riders didn't like them was because they added a bit of weight to the crash helmet, so I understood where they were coming from. But as somebody who was taking the promotion of the sport seriously it was worth getting used to the extra weight. One of the first GoPro videos that went viral was my maiden win at the Erzberg in 2013 which I'll come onto soon. As far as I know, this was the first time one of the big races had been filmed on board with a top rider before, and it was pretty cool. The viewer experienced everything I did, minus all the pain and muck! As the technology has moved on, the cameras have become lighter, and these days we've all got them. Ask any Hard Enduro fan what they enjoy most about the sport, apart from taking part or watching it live, and the vast majority will say on-board videos. We do have to edit bits out, by the way. Especially the language.

Somebody made the point the other day that despite being quiet in real life, I'm actually very active on social media. There is obviously a commercial side to this, as the likes of Instagram, Facebook and YouTube are my shop window and allow me to sell myself and show the public what I do and what I get up to. But they also allow me to communicate with my fans, which is great, and because it's all done remotely I find it a bit easier. If you notice, though, I don't tend to write a great deal on the posts, as the photos and videos tend to do most of the talking. That's my first language, really, riding a bike, and it's the one I'm most comfortable speaking.

From a personal point of view, one of the best things about GoPros is that they help to prevent journalists – or should I say some journalists – from writing inaccurate or skewed reports. That used to happen a lot in the old days, but not anymore. Some journalists used to have favourite riders, and regardless of who'd won it was them who would receive all the plaudits. Thanks to GoPro and social media, the world and his wife can now see what's happened at either a Trial or a race so there's no room for either poetic licence or favouritism.

One of the reasons I took to Hard Enduro is because it suits my personality. Generally speaking you're riding on your own, which I rather like, and when you do come into contact with another rider you're usually either passing them or helping them out. There's a great deal of camaraderie in the sport, especially during a race, and despite enjoying the solitude it's one of the things I like most. Quite often you'll see a rider taking a wrong turn, and when that happens you'll shout to them and wave them in the right direction. Don't get me wrong, everybody wants to win – that's a given – and if I saw a rider going in the wrong direction who was in danger of beating me in a race I'd keep my mouth tight shut. The camaraderie's cultural, though, and some of that comes from the fact that so many Trials riders are competing. Everyone wants to win, but nobody really wants to see anyone else fail, if that makes sense.

When Taddy signed for KTM as a factory rider, he basically became the sport's biggest star, and because none of the other manufacturers were prepared to make that kind of investment in one rider he could basically do what he wanted and was treated differently to the rest of us. Given his popularity and the age of the sport some of this was understandable, but the favouritism often went to ridiculous lengths, and as well as pissing me off a bit it made me go to some ridiculous lengths too.

I was at the Erzberg a few years ago. I'd just sold my Sherco to a mate of mine called Luke Copestake, so it must have been soon after I signed for Husaberg. I'd met Luke while I was out doing a bit of motocross, and after I sold him the Sherco he said he'd like to come out to Erzberg with me. It was still early days in the sport for me, and because we got on well I said OK.

The day before the prologue I suggested to Luke that we go and have a look at the prologue track. This was strictly against the so-called rules, by the way, and there were marshals in place to stop you doing it. This kind of thing was completely out of character for me, but the reason I decided to flout these rules was because Taddy had been driving his 4x4 all over the prologue course without anybody saying a word, so it seemed to be one rule for Taddy and one rule for everyone else. Incidentally, had I been Taddy I'd have done exactly the same, so it wasn't his fault.

Now, I'm not suggesting for one moment that the marshals were complicit in allowing Taddy to view the course, but if your name wasn't Taddy and you weren't driving a 4x4 then they would do everything in their power to stop you. That didn't prevent us from trying to have a look, though. After all, they couldn't observe the entire course all the time, so providing we were quiet and quick we might just get away with it. I just wanted to see the corners, really, so I didn't think it would be any trouble.

We managed to get away with it for about an hour, and because we were doing something we shouldn't have been we felt like naughty schoolboys. Going forward, this would become part of the traditional Erzberg challenge and was basically a game of cat and mouse.

With Husaberg looking after the bike side of things, Luke and I just had ourselves and a bit of luggage to worry about, so we'd hired ourselves a car. Well, I say a car. It was more like a hairdryer on wheels really, and I'm pretty sure the Sherco I'd sold Luke had a bigger engine.

The last bit I wanted to have a look at was the steepest part of the course, but instead of walking it we decided to take the car. In hindsight this was one of the most ludicrous things I think I have ever done in my entire life, as it was about as powerful as a rat's fart. Sure enough, after having a couple of runs at this hill we eventually got stuck and before we could extract ourselves from the course we were accosted by a very angry-looking Austrian marshal. After reversing the car to the bottom of the hill, the marshal stood in front of us so we couldn't make our escape. It was a stand-off. He was quite vocal, this bloke, and although we couldn't understand a word he was saying I'm pretty sure it wasn't *Welcome to Austria.* Unfortunately, as opposed to us being intimidated by him shouting at us we found it quite funny, and the more we tried not to laugh the more we did, and the more we laughed the angrier – and louder – this marshal became. The only word I really understood – or thought I understood – was *disqualifiziert*, which is German for disqualified. This was the word he kept on shouting again and again and again, and after the tenth time it became clear what his intentions were. *Ich werde dich disqualifizieren lassen!* – I will have you disqualified!

The only thing that really surprised me about this situation was that the marshal didn't end up having a heart attack. I wasn't too surprised we got caught and because of the Taddy situation I was ready to fight my corner. In the end this marshal actually ripped the licence plate off the hire car and then escorted us to see the race's inventor and organiser, Karl Katoch. Although I couldn't understand fully what the marshal was saying, he was obviously telling Karl that I should be excluded from the race. This put Karl in a very difficult position. While he was deciding what to do, Luke and I made our way back to base. Not long after, Karl came by and said that he had no choice but to exclude me from the race. I was disappointed about this but said fair enough. I'd made my views clear, and I couldn't do any more. A bit later on Karl came around again and said that actually I could compete. This was my final warning, though, so if I got caught again that would be it.

Since then things have changed massively and that kind of thing doesn't happen anymore. It can't, if the sport's going to succeed. That said, you're still not allowed to go and look at the course before the race, and because the rule now applies to everybody, I'm fine with it. Do riders still try and sneak on to have a look? I couldn't possibly say.

In 2012, the year after I'd won every big race except the Erzberg, I left the Flite team to become a direct factory rider for Husaberg. I'd actually signed a new three-year contract with the Flite team the year before, but unfortunately they'd started missing a few payments and everything was going sour. It was a shame, as the lads had given me a real leg up in Hard Enduro, and I was grateful to them. I still am. We'd had a hell of a successful year, and nobody will ever be able to take that away from us.

At this time, I was also dabbling in Enduro cross, a hybrid

of Trials, supercross (a variant of motocross) and Enduro, which almost always takes place in stadiums or arenas. Unlike indoor Trials, in which I had to take part no matter what, as I invariably needed the money, and the events were often part of a championship, I could kind of pick and choose with Enduro cross, and although I don't compete anymore, I've had some fun over the years. One of the first ones I did was in Las Vegas and was part of the X Games. To say it opened my eyes would be an understatement. The arena must have had at least 25,000 people in it, and because it was a race – there were three heats followed by a semi-final and a final – the atmosphere was totally different to Trials. It was louder, for a start, and there was a lot more excitement in the air. This, and the fact that we were racing, made me feel much less self-conscious than I usually did at an indoor event, and to be honest I quite enjoyed it. As with indoor Trials, the money was decent, and I'm pretty sure I ended up finishing in the top five in Vegas, so it was a good start. The eurocross event after this took place in a huge stadium in Barcelona, and to say I had an off day would be a gross understatement. With an hour and a half to go before my first race, I decided to get something to eat. I'm a sucker for a free buffet and at the indoor events they really look after you. When I was about halfway through my pasta salad, I caught a glimpse of the watch belonging to the chap sitting next to me and it said 2 p.m. *Hang on,* I thought. *My race starts at 2 p.m.*

'Excuse me,' I said to the owner while pointing at his watch. 'Is that the right time?'

'Yes,' he said. 'It's just gone 2 p.m.'

'Oh, shit! I forgot to put my watch forward from UK time.'

Fortunately, I was already in my race suit, so all I had to

do was grab my helmet, as my bike would have been taken to the start. When I finally made it to the start line, there were eleven riders and about fifty thousand people all wondering where I was.

'Sorry I'm late,' I blurted out while clambering onto my bike. 'I forgot to put my watch forward.'

Needless to say I didn't win.

On another occasion I had an accident during a race and ended up getting stretchered off. I hit a double jump wrong, winded myself, and before I knew it I was being lifted onto a stretcher and removed unceremoniously from the stadium. I think that was the first time I'd ever been stretchered off in either sport before, and there would have to be bloody cameras there. It's on YouTube somewhere.

As with Hard Enduro, as time went on the sport of Endurocross became more and more professional, and as the tracks became faster so did the riders. In that respect, it all became a bit intense for my liking as the tracks are obviously very short, so in the end I decided to concentrate on Hard Enduro instead. That's not to say I don't come out of retirement if the right offer comes along.

It took a while, but in 2013 Sonya and I managed to sort our differences, and I started to see Ellie and Jack on a regular basis again. I'd barely seen them for three years, and the first meeting was awkward to say the least. I remember us all sitting there wondering what to say, when suddenly Ellie said cheekily, 'Awkward silence, eh?', and that broke the ice and made us laugh. We've never looked back since, and it's been great making up for lost time. Sonya and I get on fine, too, so everyone's good.

The reason I'm mentioning this is because since getting close to Jack and Ellie again, they've become my main inspiration for winning. Well, that and beating my young adversaries. When I didn't see them, I used to ride as a distraction, as it was hard not to think about them. These days, I just want to make them proud of their old man.

Ellie has just started riding a Trials bike and Jack is obsessed with football. I've never pushed them and am just pleased and proud that they're having a go at something.

11

In 2013 I won the Erzberg for the first time. It brought to the end a nightmare that had started way back in 2010 and as well as denying me a grand slam or two along the way, it had played havoc with my nerves. You've heard of the saying 'third time lucky'? Well, as far as the Erzberg and me are concerned, it was fourth time lucky, and that first win came after three consecutive disqualifications. *Three!*

Given the above, and the fact that the Erzberg is the pinnacle of Hard Enduro, I've decided to give it a separate chapter, and what better place to start than at the very beginning. Or at least the very beginning of my relationship with this unique and truly incredible race.

At the time of writing, I've just won the Erzberg for a record-equalling fifth time, so, bearing in mind what I've just said, you could say I'm feeling quite pleased with myself. As the highest profile race on the Hard Enduro calendar that was a big, big win for an old man of 44, and I don't mind admitting that when I crossed the line I went ballistic. Well, as ballistic as Graham Jarvis can go. There was a time not too long ago when I thought I'd be lucky to win one Erzberg, so the fact that I've gone from there to having five under my belt is a source of great satisfaction.

The Erzberg takes my nerves to a completely new level and it was the first one of the big five I ever competed in. Talk about a baptism of fire! Funnily enough, it was also the one I managed to win last.

There are two reasons it makes me nervous. First, it's televised live in about a hundred different countries, which tends to stir things up a bit, and second, it's incredibly intense. The Hare Scramble at the end is a short race and features 500 riders in the final.

Together with Hell's Gate and Romaniacs, the Erzberg is the race that put the sport on the map, and it's held in a place called Eisenerz, which is in the Austrian Alps. This giant three-day event takes place in and around a working iron-ore quarry that produces over 2 million tonnes of the stuff every year. It's situated at the bottom of a 5,030ft mountain, which is known to the locals as the Iron Mountain (*Eisen* is German for 'iron'), and because of the way the tracks leading out of the quarry have been carved out, it tends to resemble a giant Walnut Whip!

Being situated on the edge of the Alps means the setting is pretty hard to beat. Saying that, tigers look quite nice from a distance, but you wouldn't want to ride a motorcycle over one. The same thing applies with this place, believe me.

For anyone who doesn't know, the event itself usually features around 1,800 riders, from at least forty different countries, and because of the terrain, and the fact that there are one or two motorbikes flying around, it's usually filmed from helicopters. That said, there are still about 50,000 nutcases who'll risk life and limb by watching it in person every year, and millions more tune in at home. The people watching it in person know exactly how dangerous it is, and they tend to act accordingly; i.e., like it's the last thing they'll ever do. The riders are in a similar frame of mind, only heightened, so it makes for a tense and dangerous atmosphere. Testosterone Mountain, they should call it. Seriously, the Erzberg Rodeo is unique, not just to motorcycling, but to sport.

It's hard to put into words exactly what it feels like to take part in a race like this, as the field is so vast. In 2017, only a handful finished the race; and more than 200 riders required medical attention, which is about the same as the London Marathon, whose field numbers around 40,000. The only way you can cope in a situation like that is to be acutely aware of what's going on around you without letting it overwhelm you. That's easier said than done, of course, and the first time I ever competed at the Erzberg it's fair to say that I wasn't really prepared. Then again, the only way you can truly prepare for the Erzberg is by competing in it, so you've got to start somewhere.

These days I know exactly how to prepare, but it took me the best part of a decade to learn. I mean, how on earth do you get ready for a race that involves an iron-ore quarry, a 5,030ft mountain with 50,000 nutcases scattered over it, and 1,800 riders, hundreds of whom are about to get injured? First, you learn how to block out a hell of a lot of shit. Then, after developing a superhuman pain threshold, you grow yourself an extremely large pair of testicles.

The first year I entered was 2006, so I was still riding Trials full time. There was only really Knighter who had already competed at the Erzberg, and because of what he'd told me

I thought I had the measure of it. After all, regardless of the conditions, a race is a race, right? Wrong! I'm not saying I was complacent when I arrived in Austria in 2006, but I was treating it as 'just another race'. That's all well and good if you know what's coming, but I didn't.

On the Friday and Saturday, you ride what's called the Iron Road Prologue, a 13km long gravel path that leads from the top of Iron Mountain to the summit of the quarry. The two prologues are the qualifying events for Sunday's final, and on each day you have 1,800 riders who are released individually in forty-second intervals. The final day is known as the Hare Scramble. Only the top 500 from the prologues are eligible, and the route, which is about 35km, is changed every year. The top riders require only about two and a half hours to complete the track, but if other riders manage to stay the course you could have them crossing the line anything up to two hours later. It's a sprint, though, compared to some other races.

The only advantage to my complacency prior to my first attempt at the Erzberg was that I slept like a log the night before (I still can't believe I decided to camp one year!), so in that respect my ignorance was definitely bliss. I've already touched on this, but sometimes it's OK riding when you're tired, because the knowledge that you're not firing on all cylinders can heighten your awareness. That can last only so long, however, and at races like the Erzberg you need more than just a limited supply of adrenalin to get you through. You need stamina, luck, determination, and, as I just said, a couple of large ones underneath. But none of that's any use unless you're prepared for what's to come.

The temperature back in 2006 was well over thirty degrees,

and it stayed the same for the duration of the event. I was used to riding in the heat but not in such a crammed and intense environment. The tiered starts in the final don't make much of a difference, by the way. Once you're over the start line, it's every man for himself, and for every rider who manages to stay focused and composed, you'll get a hundred who end up ploughing into the water that collects at the bottom of the quarry, or, if they manage to get out of the quarry, the dust.

The Friday and the Saturday actually went OK for me. Although tough, there are one or two straights on the prologue, and on the final stretch I managed to get up to about 90mph. That might not sound like much, but these are tracks, not roads, and there are a couple of blind crests that take some bottle to keep the throttle twisted. I admit, I almost crapped myself once or twice, but the adrenalin rush was like nothing I'd ever experienced before. This race was the closest thing to the Scott Trial I'd ever ridden, and looking back it's probably what got me hooked on Hard Enduro.

What often freaks you out during the Erzberg – and this goes for all Hard Enduros really – is that anything can happen. Anything! Ride too close to the edge of the track and you're straight down the side of a mountain. It's as simple as that. Since the race began in 1995 several people have been killed at the Erzberg – riders and spectators. That also plays on your mind. Once you know it's happened, of course. In 2015, which is one of the years I won the race, an onlooker was killed by a falling rock that had been dislodged by a bike, and that obviously overshadowed everything. Deaths are far more common at the Isle of Man TT, but they're almost always down to one thing – speed. At the Erzberg anything can get you, and that's a hell of a prospect. You could die at any moment, bike or no bike. In 2006 I had absolutely no idea about the casualties, or just how dangerous it was, which is another reason why I did well in the qualifiers. Once again, ignorance was bliss for me.

I qualified 49th for the main race, which was a big achievement for Graham 'Slowtime' Jarvis! That was down to a mixture of luck, skill – I've got to be fair to myself occasionally – and the aforementioned blissful ignorance. It was only when I lined up for the Hare Scramble that I began to appreciate just how unique the Erzberg is.

The average field in a big Hard Enduro race is about two hundred at most, so this was more than double that. The fastest qualifiers were at the front of the pack, and the slowest at the back, but regardless of which, you were all in one group and, despite being at the front-end, I was distracted slightly by what, and who, was behind me. With the sound of the engines revving, it honestly felt like I was about to be hunted down. Until then I'd always felt exhilarated by the sound of a motorcycle, never intimidated.

I was about to write that the first few seconds of the Hare Scramble are absolute chaos – which they are – but that would be doing the rest of the race a disservice. It's like *The Whacky Races* from start to finish! The race starts at the bottom of the quarry, so it's like the prologues in reverse. As you can imagine, getting five hundred riders and their bikes lined up in the bottom of a quarry is a nightmare, so although they let us into the quarry in the order in which we qualified, it's never an exact science as to who goes where. Because of the logistics involved, we're down there about two hours before the race starts so once the bikes are lined up we'll get off, stretch our legs and walk the first few hundred metres. It's good to keep busy, so as well as doing an interview for the live TV coverage I'll usually wander around and chat to some of the other riders. Amateurs, mainly. The atmosphere changes bigtime once the engines start up which is when you remember that the last two hours have been the calm before a very large oncoming storm.

When the flag drops, the bullshit stops, as Malcolm used to say, and as the signal went for the first fifty riders to start (there's about a minute gap between each group of fifty) only forty-nine set off. I was the odd one out and as the other forty-nine riders flew off towards the first corner I was still willing my 450 to fire up. 'Come on you fucker,' I started muttering. Fortunately, after a second or two, it did as it was told, and I set off flat out. In order to try and catch up I went into the first corner a bit too fast and ended up sliding sideways into another rider. After the corner, you have to try and negotiate some massive pools of water. The key here is not to get splashed as any loss of vision could be a disaster and mercifully I managed to stay out of trouble.

By the time I reached the first climb it was mayhem, and, as well as having riders falling into the side of me, I was being shunted from behind every two seconds and before me was just a sea of bikes and bodies. After finally managing to exit the quarry, I looked back and realised there must have been at least two hundred riders still in there. It's almost like another qualifying section really, as only half the field ever manage to get out. It's like spiders in a bath.

A few kilometres later I reached the first serious decline and came to an immediate halt. It must have been at least twenty-five metres down and was basically a vertical drop. In fact, I'm pretty sure it dipped in at one point and it reminded me of the end bank in the woods back in Kent, but about fifty times bigger! I asked the marshals what I was supposed to do, and they looked at me as if to say, *what the hell are you asking us for?* In the end, I laid my bike on its side, kicked it down and then followed it on my arse. I might be brave, but I'm not stupid! A few years later at Romaniacs I came to a similar kind of section that seemed impossible to scale, so instead of attempting it I put my bike into neutral, pushed it down and then slid down as carefully as I could on my arse. The bike suffered quite a bit of damage but luckily my mechanic Damo was just around the corner at the service point and had the handlebars, the subframe and the throttle changed within about twenty minutes.

About half an hour in I started passing riders who were suffering from heat exhaustion, and I remember seeing a rider trying to punch the person who'd stopped to help him. I think he'd lost the plot, as he was trying to take all his clothes off! He wasn't the only one. If you gave me a pound for every rider I've seen lying on his back with his helmet off talking to himself at the Erzberg, I'd be able to buy the quarry! It's like *Mad Max* crossed with *Armageddon*.

One of the things I remember most from the 2006 race is two spectators catching a rider after he'd fallen off his bike. This was at the top of yet another almost vertical climb and had they not caught him he'd have fallen at least two hundred feet. At the time, about 35 per cent of me was going, *What the hell are you doing here, Jarvis? Get back to Yorkshire as soon as you can and just open a shop or something!* Unfortunately, the other 65 per cent was going, *Just look at that! That's incredible.* As I said, it was a real baptism of fire, that one.

Had I not gone on to eventually conquer the Iron Giant after those three disappointments, I think I'd be residing in some kind of mental institution now, as it would have haunted me for the rest of my life. In fact, before I finally won the Erzberg for the first time – 22 June 2013 is a date that will be etched on my mind for all eternity – I'd started to doubt if I ever would. It was a win that was four years in the making and involved a lot of endeavour, a bit of politics and a few cross words.

What kept me going was the fact that I was winning everything else at the time, and I genuinely did believe that I was the best in the sport. You have to, don't you, if you're going to beat everyone else? Even so, had I not been winning so much at the time, perhaps I wouldn't have kept trying to break my duck. Then again, perhaps that's just a load of bollocks. Of course I would!

In 2010 I was disqualified for missing a checkpoint. I was fuming at the time as I'd been catching Taddy and was set for a win. It was rumoured that somebody had deliberately stood in front of an arrow in order to fix the race, but without the aid of GoPros there was no evidence. Taddy ended up winning it, and I thought, *OK, fair enough.* I just had to put it down to experience.

The following year was a completely different kettle of fish, and it may well have left some riders broken. I won the race, or at least I thought I had, and when I came over the line I felt an overwhelming sense of relief. Not because of what had happened the year before, but simply because I'd won the Erzberg! That in itself rouses emotions that you never even knew existed – or at least emotions that I never knew existed – which is all down to what it demands of you to win the race and what it takes out of you. It must be like winning an Iron Man triathlon, I suppose, just a bit quicker and in a more intense environment. There are no swims or long slow runs in this game. It's full-on, every second. As far as I'm concerned, it's the ultimate physical challenge, and the emotions that go with a win mirror that.

Once again, I'd won every other big race on the Hard Enduro calendar that year, which made winning the mighty Erzberg even more important. It was the final piece of my Hard Enduro jigsaw, and the moment I crossed the finish line – and for about twenty minutes afterwards – I thought I'd completed it. I recently watched a video of my immediate post-race reaction that day and you can tell how pleased and relieved I am. I'm almost animated! It's exactly how I remember it.

About ten minutes after the presentation ceremony, during which I'd sprayed the champagne and soaked up the glory, some of the other riders started making a fuss about something. About five minutes after that I was told by the officials that one of the marshals had said that I'd gone the wrong way, so they were awarding the victory to Taddy. I found out later that this time I definitely did mess up and had missed a five-metre climb to a checkpoint.

I don't have a lot of luck with this sort of thing as a couple of years ago at the 24MX Alestrem, which is the biggest Hard Enduro race in France, Jonny and Wade Young missed a section of the course by mistake which gave them a massive time advantage but because the organisers couldn't corroborate what had happened they were never penalised, and it ended up costing me £5,000 in prize money!

It's difficult to explain the emotions I felt immediately after the race in 2011 and if I don't watch myself I'll be in danger of sounding like a bitter old man. For the first hour or so I wanted to punch somebody. The main thing was that I knew I was capable of winning and I had to look at the positives. That made it five on the bounce for Taddy, and in my eyes I should have had at least two of them. I felt extremely hard done by and anybody would have felt the same. The following day I'd calmed down a bit, and although I was still desperately disappointed I no longer wanted to punch anybody and was back to thinking Taddy was a good lad, which he is. I knew that the press and fans would still be talking about it, but that didn't bother me. All that bothered me was how I would respond to what had happened, and, like so many times before, I realised I just had to crack on. The Erzberg would still be there next year, but I couldn't help wondering if it would ever happen.

In 2012 I won Romaniacs, Hell's Gate, the Sea to Sky and the Tough One – together with one or two other races – so I was more determined than ever to win the Erzberg. But because of what had happened the year before, I was even more self-conscious than usual when I arrived in Austria. I was also the red-hot favourite, so it's fair to say that when the event started all eyes were on me.

I made quite a fast start, which was unusual for me, but immediately ran into trouble on the first climb, and after crashing into a fallen rider I became involved in a multi-bike pile-up that must have taken place no more than a few hundred metres from the start. Those riders who were in front of the crash managed to open up a gap, and just to make things worse I'd injured my wrist, although I was able to carry on. Typical!

Once I was free of the pile-up, I set about catching the leaders and, after steadily working my way through the traffic I managed to get myself into the top five. Then, in an attempt to reach the leaders, I apparently missed out a section of the track. I only missed about two corners, so it wasn't exactly a lot and because I had no idea what had happened I just carried on. In hindsight, it was probably poor visibility that did it for me, as the upper half of the mountain was covered in low cloud, and I simply failed to see the track markings. I was riding with Andi Lettenbichler when it happened and once he realised we'd missed it, the marshal warned the other riders so they didn't do the same. Lucky them!

Still oblivious to what had happened, I just focused on reeling in the leaders, and by checkpoint 13, which is Carl's Diner, I was in second place. After finding a fast line through the next section of the course I was able to greatly reduce Jonny Walker's lead before catching him during a forestry climb shortly before the next checkpoint. After that, I pushed as hard as I possibly could to build a lead, and when I crossed the line I experienced a watered-down version of everything I'd felt the previous year. With all the low cloud and the crash at the beginning, I was very nervous about my result, and, sure enough, seconds after crossing the line my worst fears were confirmed. For the third time in a row I had crossed the line first only to be disqualified. The only bonus this time was that it happened before I had a chance to celebrate, so I had less of a fall. The live camera zoomed in on my face as Karl was telling me. It was like a kid being told that Christmas was cancelled. 'Unbelievable', I said, before going to the van to sulk.

After working so hard to recover from the crash, I was gutted to have lost the race, but I had to look at the positives. My recovery, in particular, gave me an awful lot of heart, and despite the mistake and the eventual result I was pleased with how I'd ridden. The next race on the calendar was Romaniacs, and I'd head there determined to make amends. The only question was, would I be able to perform at the same level at next year's Erzberg? Three disqualifications, though. I was beginning to think – quite seriously, sometimes – that somebody on that bloody mountain had it in for me.

What annoyed me most at the 2012 race wasn't so much the mistake, as that Jonny had won. Don't get me wrong. I get on well with Jonny and he's a very talented rider. Although we're not best mates or anything, we do text each other occasionally, and there's a hell of a lot of mutual respect. At the time, though, Jonny was being touted as the next big thing in Hard Enduro, and this was his first major win in the sport. It would have to be the one race I hadn't won myself, wouldn't it?

In 2013, which was the first time I ever used a GoPro at the Erzberg, the pressure was on and all the talk prior to the race was about the battle between me and Jonny. I had an absolute nightmare on the prologue, and I ended up qualifying on the second row. I'm not sure if anyone had ever won the race from the second row before, but while it wasn't considered to be impossible, it was definitely one hell of a task.

Part of the reason for me struggling (although I have to admit it was only a very small part) was that I was trying out some new electric goggles at the time which were supposed to work the roll-off system at the touch of a button.

The conditions were desperate, and the water just after the start was half a metre deep in places. As I rode, waves of water started lapping over me and for a few moments I couldn't see a thing. Suddenly I remembered my new goggles so activated them and hoped for the best. Miraculously they actually worked and as well as being able to see the climb out of the quarry, which was handy, there was a clear line.

The thing I remember most about this race, apart from the conditions, is the paranoia. I felt all right before the start, but my three previous disqualifications were now beginning to prey on my mind, and despite the good start I was terrified about missing a checkpoint or making any kind of mistake. Although I was expected to compete in the Erzberg, I'm not sure I could have carried on for year after year. I *had to win* this bloody race.

When I rode towards the tyres just before the finish line, I allowed myself a little wheelie. Given what had happened in the past, this could have been tempting fate, but after taking the lead at the halfway stage, I was going to be the first over the line, providing I didn't fall off and knock myself out. I was also sure that I'd completed the course cleanly. And I had.

Even when Karl Katoch, who is the founder of the Erzberg Rodeo, confirmed to me that I'd won the race I still didn't believe him. I didn't tell him that, but while everybody was handing me flags to wave and patting me on the back I was still expecting a tap on the shoulder.

'Excuse me, Graham. Could I have a word with you, please? We've got some bad news.'

If that had happened again, I think I'd have taken up flower-arranging or something. Even in the car on the way home it didn't feel real.

I'd ridden the Erzberg knowing that I was the best rider in the field several times before and although just completing the race is an achievement, knowing you're the best but not winning is like having a permanent itch. You can only truly relax and be happy when that itch has gone. Fortunately, I managed to scratch mine. Eventually!

Since breaking my duck, I've managed to win the Erzberg four times, in 2015, 2016, 2018 and 2019. In 2015 I shared the title with three other riders after we helped each other through some extraordinarily tough terrain.

The section prior to the finish line, which is called Downtown, was new to the race and included a huge gully in a seemingly impassable stretch of forest. We were able to get through this gully only by pulling together, and after more than an hour of backbreaking teamwork the four of us – me, Jonny Walker, Alfredo Gómez and Andreas Lettenbichler – crossed the line side by side after precisely four hours of racing. It was the first time anything like this had happened at the Erzberg and we were applauded over the finish line by a huge and very vocal crowd. I don't think I've ever been as tired in my life.

In contrast to this, and to my first win in 2013, my win in 2016 was textbook and was one of those days when everything just fell into place. In that respect it's safe to say

I've experienced pretty much everything at the Erzberg. Certainly every emotion. Then again, the Erzberg has everything: the views, the terrain, the spectacle, the cachet, the pain! It really is the ultimate test.

12

From 2011 onwards I've spent a lot of my time competing in and talking about Hard Enduro's big six races. In calendar order, they are the Tough One, which takes place in January, Hell's Gate, which takes place in February, the Erzberg, which takes place at the end of May and/or early June, Romaniacs, which is in July, the Sea to Sky, which is in October, and the Roof of Africa, which takes place in December. Because they're all so different, I've decided to give the four events I haven't mentioned much yet – The Tough One, Romaniacs, Sea to Sky and the Roof of Africa – a section of their own. Hopefully this will help to bring them all to life a bit.

THE TOUGH ONE

When the Tough One, which takes place in Oswestry on the Welsh border, first started back in 2005, it was just like all the other Hard Enduro races, in that it was something the Enduro boys such as Knighter did in their spare time and had been for a few years. Nobody really specialised in it, though, and because there were no specialists, nobody took it all that seriously. That all started to change once the prize money got a bit better, and as more top Enduro riders entered Hard Enduro races the standard improved. It was a genuine snowball effect and ultimately it was those boys who helped to put Hard Enduro on the map. What took it to another level was when Trials riders like me and Dougie started dabbling, and from 2009 onwards its growth has been exponential.

Although he's known for Enduro mainly, Knighter, who also started off in Trials, was one of the first riders to get behind Hard Enduro, and because of his profile he drew a lot of interest. By the time people like Dougie and I started competing, it was starting to gain a following, but in truth I think that was as much to do with the excitement of the sport as it was because of our participation. We just gave it a leg up. That said, in order for Hard Enduro to work as a spectacle you have to have riders who make it look easy, or at least easier. They're the ones who make the spectators watch on with open mouths.

As well as being the UK's premier Hard Enduro race, the Tough One was one of the first I ever competed in. Or at least the first that wasn't a local race. It was a very different animal back then and has grown massively over the years.

I think Knighter must have lapped me at least twice in 2006, my first year in the race. I was riding the Sherco 450 four-stroke and didn't really have a clue what I was doing. The speed was absolutely ridiculous, and the gulf between the likes of Knighter and me was vast. I used to watch Knighter a lot in those early days and have learned more from him than anyone else (he'll probably send me an invoice now!). It was his speed that used to impress me the most. He really was the benchmark.

I sometimes wonder what might have happened with Knighter had he moved over to Hard Enduro permanently. When I said that he specialised in Hard Enduro, what I really meant to say was that he set an early standard for everyone else to follow. Or at least he helped to. After that he went back to Enduro and did a lot of stuff in the USA. Successfully, I might add. Although he's dabbled in Hard Enduro since then, he hasn't managed to replicate that early form. Yet! Mr Knight is three years younger than me, so I wouldn't write him off just yet.

Instead of finding that first race intimidating, as I might have done in Trials, it motivated me, and I just saw it as a challenge. For a start, I knew I was on the wrong bike, and despite getting a thumping and being lapped by Knighter I really enjoyed myself. It was a good starting point. The Tough One wasn't nearly as big as it is now, but then neither was the sport. In fact, I think Hard Enduro was in just the right place for me when I started to make the switch, and because it was a young sport I was able to grow with it. Had it been more advanced I might have struggled, so I was lucky in that respect.

One of the things I enjoy about the Tough One – and again, I'm not sure this would have been the same in Trials – is the fact that it's a home crowd. As I've mentioned before, one of the reasons I perhaps didn't fulfil my potential in Trials is because the spectators are in such close proximity to the riders – sometimes for long periods of time – and that used to make me feel uncomfortable. Some people find it easy to block them out, but because I was naturally shy and a bit nervous I found it difficult. It's certainly not the only reason, as I've already made clear, but it was a factor. In Hard Enduro you occasionally have that close proximity but because you're moving quickly it doesn't matter. The spectators are there and then they're gone.

The worst part about the rider/spectator relationship in Trials – for me, at least – was messing up a section because if I did make a hash of something the spectators would fall silent. It wasn't the silence itself that I found unnerving, it was the knowledge of why it had happened. I used to take the whole thing quite personally, which was a shame really because in reality their silence wasn't a reflection of the fans' disapproval. Yes, they were disappointed that I'd made a mistake, but that was only because they wanted to see the section cleared. It wasn't a personal vendetta or anything.

My first Tough One, in which you have to ride as many laps as you can in three hours around Nantmawr Quarry and over some pretty testing obstacles and terrain, was the biggest Hard Enduro race I'd ever been involved in on home soil, and the atmosphere was new and invigorating. There must have been at least a couple of thousand people scattered around the course, and the mood certainly matched the action. It was frenetic. Something that adds to this energy is that instead of starting the race on their bikes, the riders have to run up a hill first, then get on their bikes and set off hell for leather. Even back in 2006 I was probably one of the oldest riders in the field so instead of busting a gut by trying to match all the twenty-year-olds I just did my usual thing of hanging back and playing the long game. The hill is usually quite muddy, as is much of the course, so it probably looks quite comical. But it creates a massive amount of tension, and although I'm not overly keen on a running start it's great for the spectators.

Although he won in 2006 (and in 2005, 2007 and 2008!), Knighter had a bit of a nightmare start that year. He heard the bikes start up and thought the race had begun without him. Without stopping to check, he ran up the hill to get to his bike, but when he got there it was just the Clubman riders warming theirs up. He had to walk back down the hill again, and because the race then started almost immediately he was knackered! According to Knighter he couldn't really get going until the third or fourth lap because he was in among so many riders and later on his rear wheel jammed after getting a rock stuck in it. The fact that he still went on to win just proves how dominant he was back then, and despite him lapping me I managed to finish fourth, which I was pleased with.

Because it takes place at the beginning of the year the Tough One can get really, really muddy, and I suppose this has played into my hands over the years. Some of the hill climbs can get really treacherous and you've got bikes and riders flying everywhere.

The first time I won the race was in 2011, by which time it had moved to the Back Cown Quarry near Manchester, but only for a year or two. Fortunately I was no stranger to the new venue, and although I was confident going into it I wasn't looking forward to the Le Mans-style running start. I'd have been almost thirty-eight by then, so I should have asked somebody for a piggy back!

I thought I'd managed to hobble to my bike pretty quickly, but all of the other riders seemed to start faster than I did, and I think I was second to last out, which wasn't what I wanted. All I had to do was remind myself that it was a three-hour race and not to do anything stupid on the first lap.

Despite suffering with crippling arm pump, I was soon back in contact with early race leader Andreas Lettenbichler, and despite some unexpected good weather making the course a little bit easier there were still a few places where the riders were forced to get off and push.

After managing to work my way past most of the other riders during the first half of the opening lap, I was able to overtake Lettenbichler, but the arm pump prevented me from riding as hard as I wanted to, which maybe wasn't such a bad thing. At the end of the first hour, I think I was less than two minutes ahead, so I started to put in a few quick laps. My arm had calmed down a bit by this point, and during the second hour I managed to open up a commanding lead. I'd had some pretty bad luck in some of the previous Tough Ones, and I remember thinking to myself that this was going to be a sweet win.

Then, just as I approached the last thirty minutes I hit a wall. Not a real one, but a physiological one, as in I just didn't have the strength to keep going. It doesn't matter how fit you are, sometimes your body will just say no, and it can be for any number of different reasons. To be honest, I couldn't put my finger on anything at the time, and rather than wondering why it had happened, I needed to fight against it. Had there been riders within a few seconds of me I might just have given up the ghost, but with only a few spectators dotted around I was able to give each obstacle my full concentration – or what was left of it – and just pray that I managed to hang on. At the end of the day, a win is only worth so much, and sometimes you have to put safety first. Given what I do for a living, that might sound a bit daft, but in order to take part in a dangerous sport you need to be physically able, and if you're not, you become a liability. The reason people watch dangerous sports is because they enjoy seeing their heroes defy the odds, and if they happen to go arse over tit in the process, it should not be because they aren't up to it.

By the time I was into the last ten minutes I was wobbling like a four-year-old who'd just had his stabilisers removed, and I think the last lap, which was purgatory, took more out of me than the previous twenty combined. Although there weren't really any places to get stuck, there was nowhere to take a rest, and not really anywhere that you could grab a quick drink either. I was definitely pleased to see the finish.

Between 2011 and 2019 I haven't lost once at the Tough One, and although there are people out there who think it shouldn't be considered as one of the big six, I most certainly do.

ROMANIACS

After chalking up six victories at Romaniacs, I'm now known to some Romanian fans as – wait for it – *The King of the Carpathians!* I'll settle for that.

The Romaniacs takes place in the Carpathian Mountains (or at least most of it does), and it lasts an exhausting five days. The race consists of an inner-city prologue on day one, and then four days in the mountains. Don't assume that by mountains I mean rocky tracks. The Carpathian mountains are quite green in places, and there's a huge amount of woodland, which is some of the race's toughest terrain. One of the reasons I tend to do well is because experience really helps, and I have quite a lot of that.

Romaniacs is part of the Red Bull Hard Enduro Series, which also includes Minas Riders in Brazil in April, the Erzberg, the Sea to Sky and the Roof of Africa. I'll come on to the last two in a moment. In 2018 Romaniacs also became part of the World Enduro Super Series, which is becoming very popular. I'm afraid the WESS arrived a little bit late for me, and from a Husqvarna point of view we're represented by several riders in the series, including Billy Bolt, who, as well as being about twelve years old, is the current champion. He's a good lad is Billy.

Because of the length of the race, people often ask me how I prepare for Romaniacs, and the last time I gave an interview about it I said by getting plenty of sleep and having a good feed, specifically Ready Brek! That's always been my favourite, and one of the reasons I love it is because it's made of oats, so is full of slow-release energy, yet is easier to make than porridge. I also make sure I top up on sleep before the race starts, and I don't stay up too late after the prologue either. Each off-road day starts at 6.30 a.m., so that means I might be awake from 4.30, and after two days in the mountains that really burns on you. When I finish each day, I try to get a two-hour sleep in the afternoon to recover. Eating breakfast at 4.30 a.m. is almost impossible, so I take my Ready Brek with me.

You need to be fit, injury free and mentally strong to compete at Romaniacs, as you do with all the races on the calendar. These days one of the races prior to Romaniacs is the Trèfle Lozérien AMV, which is part of the WESS. Although it's not really my type of event, it's great preparation for Romania. It includes three long and physical days on the bike. Each day is unique, and as well as riding over new terrain you're also covering over 600 kilometres in total. Last year the race took place just four days after the Erzberg, which was another three days of hard racing, so if you factor in the test walking I often do in France around this time I'm more than ready for Romania. Well, as ready as I can be. I don't think you could ever be 'more than ready' for Romaniacs.

Because of the length of the races, and the fact that they're quite close geographically, people sometimes assume that Romaniacs and Erzberg are similar, but in truth they're worlds apart. Romaniacs is such a different animal than the Erzberg. You're alone for so much of it, riding unknown terrain and on instinct. At the Iron Giant you can do a lot of preparation for the main race, but in Romania that's not possible. You can prepare, but not on the specifics of the race.

Over the last decade the Romaniacs has evolved massively, and each day is becoming more and more intense. In the past you could afford to have a bad section or two, but now you've got to be sharp all of the time. That said, you also need to know when to push at 85 or 90 per cent and when 70 per cent will do. That comes from experience mainly. These days I always try to have a strong opening day in the mountains but leave a little in reserve. That helps me judge where everyone else is at, which is important. You don't want to lose much time on day one.

In 2018 they introduced two overnight bivouacs (temporary camps) which took us away from the host city of Sibiu to the nearby town of Petroşani. That really gave the race a kind of rally feel and was a great idea. It's good to see the organisers of these races keeping things fresh. It also means we have new tracks to ride, and although it's not good for me personally, in that I know the old terrain very well, it levels the playing field a bit.

Incidentally, when you take part in Romaniacs it's always best to take some money with you when you ride, because if the locals help you out they usually expect a few Romanian leu in return. It only really happens in the very rural areas, and because they're the only people there that makes them more or less indispensable. It's the same with the Roof of Africa, which is held in Lesotho. People living in rural areas often have very little money in places like Romania and Lesotho, so a few blokes stranded on motorbikes can be a nice little earner. Over the years they've learned how to make the most of this, and they know exactly where the riders are most likely to encounter difficulty. They're not daft.

I managed to win first time out at Romaniacs back in 2008, having travelled over there with a mate of mine called Nick Rowbottom. He was taking a van with three other bikes and very kindly offered me a lift. Had he not done so I wouldn't have been able to afford to get there and back, so in the grand scheme of things he did me a massive favour. Nick also had a mechanic with him who helped me out, so I was sorted.

Although Romaniacs is now massive, I hadn't heard much about it back then, so I didn't really know what I was getting into. That was the story of my life at the start of my Hard Enduro career. Back then the track wasn't very well marked, so I had one or two navigational issues. Saying that, GPS systems were rubbish back then, so it's a wonder anybody finished. I ended up following the German rider Gerhard Foster, who was riding a BMW, for much of the race. He seemed to know both where he was going and what he was doing, so I latched onto him like a limpet. I was better on the extreme stuff than Gerhard, but he could navigate so I'd fly up a hill or whatever and just wait for him. Right, where to next, Gerhard? I was so scared of getting lost.

He probably thinks it's funny now (or at least I hope he does), but at the time Gerhard was a bit pissed off having me around, because at the end of each day, once I'd got my bearings, I'd shoot off and try to win. Had it not been for Gerhard, I'd probably still be lost in Romania somewhere, so I owe him a drink. And a thank you!

I remember the race finished on top of a building that year and the final stretch was a gable roof with a massive drop either side. Taking that into account, it probably wasn't the safest place to pull a wheelie, but I did. I couldn't resist. You see, that's what I mean about me doing most of my talking on a bike. Had it been a race involving pushbikes or just running, you'd have been lucky to get a wave out of me. Put me on a motorbike, however, and I'll give you the world, mate!

Before I forget, there's another Hard Enduro event in Romania called King of the Hill. One year, the week before the race, Paul Bolton and I went out there to test our bikes and ended up having a drag race to see which machine had the most power. I ended up pulling in front of Paul, but when I eased off he flew by, and as he did he hit me on the elbow, knocking me off. After sliding for about twenty metres, I finally came to a halt. The road we were on wasn't exactly smooth, and I must have grazed about half my body. There was blood and skin everywhere! After an understandably painful night with not much sleep, I tried to start the race, but it was no good. My shoulder especially was absolutely red raw, so a three-day race wouldn't have been possible.

After my initial win, I had a couple of crap years in Romaniacs. In 2009, Paul Bolton took my bike over, but because I didn't have a mechanic, I ended up preparing it myself and came nowhere. It was a similar situation in 2010 when I had a stinker. It's madness when you think about it. We were all privateers, though, and the majority of us were skint. I came back in 2011, and on my way to winning six – so far – I managed to bag three in a row.

In 2018 I was all set to make it seven, but I had to pull out of the race midway, which is something I've only had to do a handful of times in my entire career. After a fun but forgettable prologue (from a result point of view), I finished fourth on the opening day and was seventeen minutes behind the leaders. I certainly hadn't ridden well, but I was also lacking energy for some reason.

Despite the lack of energy, I managed to battle through the second day, and by the halfway point I was lying fourth overall, having finished seventh on the day. On paper that didn't look too bad, but I was over thirty minutes down on the leader, Wade Young. Given how I was feeling, I was going to have a hell of a job turning things around.

I started the penultimate day feeling no better really: I felt lacklustre and was becoming increasingly tired. After reaching the first checkpoint, I was forced to withdraw from the race before the midday service point. Deciding to stop was one of the hardest things I'd ever had to do, but it was the most sensible option. I simply had no more energy to continue, and had I carried on I would almost certainly have injured myself and perhaps other people. Right from the off, I just wasn't feeling right. I wasn't feeling ill or anything, I was just inexplicably out of sorts, and didn't get into that groove like I normally do. I was also struggling in places where I knew I shouldn't have been, which made me feel frustrated. I really wanted to challenge for a seventh Romaniacs win, but it wasn't to be.

Pulling out of the odd race might not seem like much to some people, but to the riders who do it day in day out it's devastating. Especially when it's one of the big races. It might be different if it weren't so punishing, but you really do have to put everything you've got into a race like Romaniacs and if you fall short of what's required, for whatever reason, it gets to you.

I've been trying to think of the most bizarre thing that's ever happened to me at Romaniacs and unfortunately mine is a less than glamorous memory. After the race the organisers check your GoPro to make sure everything's in order and one year I'd had to stop for a crap. The thing is, I forgot to switch off my GoPro, so when the media guys were going through mine they had the pleasure of joining me for a number two. I ended up losing that race by two minutes, which is roughly the time it took me to go. Some people lose by a lap, I lost by a crap.

I've won Romaniacs with three different manufacturers, on a two-stroke and a four-stroke, and now against two generations of riders. Even though I've accomplished everything I ever wanted to in the race, I just love coming back to Romania and riding there. It's an amazing place, and one where I feel at my best, which I guess is why I've been so successful. A seventh win is the target, but I'm not going to think about that too much yet.

SEA TO SKY

When Martin Freinademetz, who is the mastermind behind Romaniacs, decided to launch a new race in 2011, anybody who had anything to do with Hard Enduro wanted to know what he had in mind. The clue is often in the name when it comes to these races, and when you heard the name Sea to Sky you definitely had a good idea what you were going to be up against.

It first took place in 2011 in the city of Kemer in Turkey. I was with Husaberg at the time, and I had to negotiate with them to be allowed to go. Because it was a new race, they weren't particularly keen, and I don't think they had the funding from their owners, KTM. In the end, they said no, but because I was so keen I went to see Martin Freinademetz. He wanted me to take part and said I could borrow a press bike, which was better than nothing.

Fortunately I wasn't the only rider who was excited about this new race, and in the end Martin managed to get a good field together. We had Chris Birch, who'd won the Roof of Africa several times, young Jonny Walker, who was starting to make his mark, Xavi Galindo, Darryl Curtis and my old mate Andreas Lettenbichler. There were about a hundred riders in all and from all over the world, so it was a good effort.

Day one (of two) kicked off with two consecutive qualifying heats. The first, which was a beach race, attracted about 3,000 spectators – many of whom were wearing nothing but bikinis. Although exciting, Hard Enduro isn't the most glamorous sport on earth, and although it was quite nice being surrounded by scantily clad women, as opposed to just mechanics and spectators wearing puffer jackets, it got a little bit distracting after a while! After the two heats, we had the forest race, which took us onto a scenic but also tiring 35km lap through Kemer's backcountry. Starting again on the beach, the track went through the town and up into the forest. The single trails that followed were challenging enough and along the way there were some riverbeds and a couple of pretty steep downhills. It wasn't the most difficult course I'd ever ridden, but the backdrop was amazing, and the tagline, 'The Most Enjoyable Hard Enduro', which I actually started, was beginning to come true.

The majority of us pro riders didn't push too hard, as all we were trying to do was make it into the top ten and so get us on the first row for the second day, which was the Olympos Mountain Race. Chris Birch won the first day, Jonny was second and I was third.

One thing I really liked about the Sea to Sky was that they'd split the race into three categories depending on your ability. This meant that rather than a load of people failing early on, which is what usually happened in Hard Enduro races, everybody had a very good chance of making it to the end, albeit to a finish that matched their ability.

The course was split into gold, silver and bronze and each was measured by altitude. If you reached 600m, you got bronze, if you made it to 1,700m, you were awarded silver, and if you got to 2,365m, which is the height of Mount Olympos, you achieved gold. Bronze was for the majority of riders, silver for the more experienced riders and gold for the rest of us. It's a really good concept, but you couldn't implement it at every race. The Erzberg, for instance, is a lot more chaotic than the Sea to Sky, and I'm sure that if you asked the majority of riders whether they'd like to aim for something less than the pro riders they'd tell you where to go. It takes a special kind of nutcase to ride the Erzberg.

I'm afraid that first year at the Sea to Sky is a bit of a hazy memory. What I do know is that only twelve riders made it to the top of Mount Olympos, and luckily I was the first. I also remember seeing the chequered flag, and when it came into view I treated myself to a bit of a wheelie. It's always great to win a race, but to win a brand-new race, and one that had been designed by the genius that is Martin Freinademetz, was terrific. Jonny had been leading for the majority of the race, but when the track started to become more technical I think his inexperience started to show a bit, and I managed to catch up and pass him. I had a feeling things might pan out like this, so I'd been happy to sit back and take my time. Chris Birch came in third. I think he had managed to pass Xavi Galindo about fifty metres from the finish, so he was very happy.

In 2013 it was an all-British affair, with me, Jonny and Paul Bolton on the podium. We're all very different personalities. I'm quiet, Jonny's slightly less so, and Paul never stops bloody talking or smiling. He's one of the biggest characters in Hard Enduro and is another one who's defying his age and giving the young ones a run for their money. Poor old Xavi Galindo came fourth again, so he must have been gutted.

I think the best win I've ever had at the Sea to Sky – so far – was in 2014. After finishing second to me in 2011 and 2012 Jonny had been on a mission in 2013, and he dominated the entire weekend. I came within striking distance once or twice towards the end of the race, but Jonny was having none of it, and every time I exerted a bit of pressure he responded. Fair play to him. We were both so knackered by the end of that race that Jonny christened it the Battle of the Deadest. He was absolutely spot on.

My preparation for the 2014 Sea to Sky was unlike anything I'd ever undertaken. I'd made quite a few mistakes in 2013, which wasn't like me, and because they'd been plaguing me – and because I wanted to win – I'd been analysing them for weeks. This paid off in the end, and although Jonny took the lead in the final race, which was nothing unusual, I was right behind him. I'm not sure if that made Jonny nervous or not, but he eventually made a mistake, and I was able to pass him. Once that had happened it was goodnight Vienna. Or, hello Olympos. That was a sweet victory. Partly because I'd beaten Jonny, but also because I'd righted a few cock-ups in the process.

Since then I've only failed to win the Sea to Sky twice. In 2016 the Austrian rider Lars Enöckl won it, but Jonny and I didn't take part that year, so it doesn't count! Then, in 2018, Jonny won it again, so the less said about that the better.

Will I have another go in 2019? Well, I can't have Mr Walker beating my record, and until they start introducing bikini-clad women at the other races I'll have to grin and bear it.

ROOF OF AFRICA

The Roof of Africa, also known as the Mother of Hard Enduro, has been going for donkey's years, but until recently it was classed as a desert race, like the Dakar Rally, rather than Hard Enduro, and featured motorbikes and cars. Since dumping the four-wheelers and making the switch it's become one of the hardest but most impressive races on the calendar. That said, it's not the fastest race there is but one of the most difficult to cope with mentally. It's a real war of attrition.

In order to get to Lesotho, a tiny mountain kingdom within the borders of South Africa, with a population of just 2 million that was under British colonial rule until the mid-1960s, you have to fly to Johannesburg first, and from there it's about a three-hour drive. Although I would class myself as being fairly well travelled, going there for the first time was a real eye-opener. Before I got on the plane bound for Joburg, I'd never heard of Lesotho. However, because it's a mountain kingdom, it's tailor-made for our sport, and the event is heavily backed by the Lesotho government, so it's well run, well attended and well funded.

The prologue for the Roof of Africa is called Around the Houses, and it's a perfect name, as that's exactly what it entails – three laps around the centre of the capital as fast as you can possibly go. These days the time it takes you to get around is added to your overall time, but in my first year it wasn't, so I just cruised around the course. It was just a spectacle then and was designed to entertain the locals. Prologues have never been my speciality anyway, so as long as I qualify in the top five or six, I'm happy.

The terrain during the race itself is different to any other race and so is the weather. You remember I said the Scottish Six Days Trial was a bit unpredictable in that department? Well, compared to the Roof of Africa it's like a week in the Canaries. During the nine hours of riding, you can experience anything from brutal heat and dust to continuous driving rain, and if the weather gods are in a particularly bad mood, it can become bitterly cold and you might even encounter snow flurries.

It's considered to be one of the most important off-road events in the southern hemisphere, and because of the altitudes involved it's very unpredictable. The race passes through the Maloti mountains, which reach heights of over 3,000 metres, and a lot of the time you're riding on goat tracks that have probably been there for decades if not centuries. This means that there are always a lot of loose rocks flying around, and because it's such a long race – nine hours a day for three days and while you're riding you don't get a break – it's easy to lose concentration. Especially towards the end. I've known riders forget to fill up their camel packs with fluids along the way, and when that happens you're in deep, deep trouble. The one time I forgot it cost me the race and was probably the most uncomfortable experience I've ever had on two wheels. How I forgot in the first place I have absolutely no idea, but when I realised what I'd done I started to panic a bit. I'd heard all kinds of horror stories about riders collapsing and crashing due to dehydration, and I thought I was about to become the latest casualty. I started to make silly mistakes, and as time went on I found it more and more difficult to focus. I also felt extremely sick, and had the race gone on for half an hour longer, I'd have been in serious trouble. I had been in the lead, but when I became dehydrated and started to make mistakes two riders passed me and I ended up finishing third.

It's such a brutal race, and if something like dehydration doesn't get you, navigation issues might. Instead of having flags along the route, they just paint arrows on rocks.

Sometimes these rocks become dislodged and when that happens you're obviously in trouble. This is where the locals really come into their own, and if they're not around and your sat nav isn't working, you could find yourself with a real problem. Tactically, it's always good to stay close to another rider if you can, because if you end up getting lost, you'll have more chance of getting yourself out of the you-know-what. I don't mind having a couple of races where you have to use sat navs and the like, but I couldn't be doing with it in every race. It'd get on my nerves.

I remember drowning my bike one year, and when it happened I was literally on my own and miles from anywhere. I was in the lead at the time, so didn't have the benefit of seeing what riders ahead of me had done. I came across some water in the bottom of a valley, and because it didn't look too deep I decided to ride through it rather than around it. It didn't go over my head or anything, but it was deep enough to drown my bike. After coming to a halt I started looking around me, and all I could see were hills and mountains. And water, of course. There was plenty of that. A few minutes later a local man walked up and helped me remove my bike. He seemed to appear out of nowhere, which was strange, and after turning my bike upside down I let nature – or in this case gravity – take its course. When the other riders finally appeared, they took one look at me and promptly drove around the water so at least I'd provided them with a service. Luckily for me the German rider Andreas Lettenbichler stopped and gave me a spark plug, so I was soon on my way again. It was a nice gesture and fairly typical of him. He's one of the few riders in Hard Enduro who is even older than I am, and he too started his career in Trials. As well as winning the Erzberg in 2015,

Andreas's son Manny finished third in the 2018 Roof behind me and Jonny. It's strange competing against two generations of the same family, and what makes it worse is that they're both talented and both very competitive.

Local riders usually do quite well at the Roof, and in 2012 the South African Wade Young won the race at just sixteen years of age. That was obviously an amazing achievement, and Wade's gone on to win the Roof of Africa four times.

My most eventful Roof of Africa, or at least one of them, took place in 2016 when I won the race for the fourth time. The reason it's so memorable is because it culminated in one of the closest finishes I've ever battled for in Hard Enduro. After battling it out over three days and almost thirty hours, I managed to beat Alfredo Gómez by just thirteen seconds. It was just like one of the races on *Top Gear*, except this was real!

After a pretty bad Round the Houses, I ended up qualifying in seventeenth. That was obviously an awful start, but I managed to redeem myself by posting the fastest time in day one's time Trial and finished the opening day of three in second place behind Yamaha's Brett Swanepoel.

On day two it was Alfredo who set the pace. His first day had been just like my Around the Houses, and he'd ended it ten minutes off the pace. That seemed to galvanise him, though, and he attacked hard to pull the time back. Subsequently, it was Alfredo who clocked the fastest time on day two, and he drew within twenty seconds of me, setting up a winner-takes-all finish on the third and final day.

On day three, Alfredo and I rode pretty much side-by-side. It was just so difficult to open up a gap. I guess that was good for both of us, as we were helping each other with navigation, but all the time I was thinking, *When's he going to make a break for it?* One of us had to win. I forget exactly where this happened but towards the end Alfredo suddenly lit things up a bit in an attempt to pip me to the post. I was ready for him, though. Because I hadn't been able to open up a gap on him I'd been preparing myself for a sprint finish. The only thing that worried me was whether I had the energy for it. Fortunately for me, Alfredo was about as exhausted as I was, and I managed to hold him off, using some of my vast experience and a little bit of good timing. A thirteen-second victory, though. That really is squeaky bum time.

A short while after the race had ended, word got round that a South African rider called Willie-John le Hanie had sustained fatal injuries on his way to the finish, giving the Roof of Africa its first fatality in more than half a century. This was obviously incredibly sad, and a minute's silence was held for him at the prize-giving ceremony in the evening. It's difficult to celebrate after something like that, but at least Willie had died doing something he loved.

Since 2016 I've had podiums but no more wins at the Roof of Africa, and I'm not sure how long I can carry on competing in the event. It's a long old journey to Lesotho, and those goat tracks are a killer. Don't write me off just yet though.

13

Now I'm an old man I tend to get asked to do more documentaries and ambassadorial stuff, and nine times out of ten they take place overseas. I said earlier in the book that I enjoy visiting new places and because they're new places they tend to provide me with new and different experiences. One of the more bizarre things that has happened to me took place on the south-east Asian island of Borneo a few years ago when I was invited to take part in a race out there. Although they call it a race, it's more of an event, really, as there are no winners and over 2,000 people take part. Motorbikes are the main mode of transport on Borneo and the entire male population seems to be obsessed by them, none more so than the Governor of the island, who is basically the man in charge.

Because of the size and significance of this event the press had come from all around, and the Governor was turning up to launch it and have his photo taken. As is often the way with the most important people, the Governor was the last man to arrive. He asked me if I'd like to ride with him, and I presumed he meant for the photos. I said yes and we set off on this track with the Governor and his men in front and me behind. After about five minutes the Governor and his men suddenly turned off the track and the next thing I know we were riding up a ravine in two feet of water. This wouldn't have been that strange had the Governor and his men been dressed for the occasion, but they were all wearing suits and shoes, and as the vegetation surrounding the ravine became thicker the Governor's men pulled out machetes and started clearing the way! The Governor even fell off at one point and they had to drag him out of the water. I think it's the only time I've ever ridden a Hard Enduro without any warning, and it's certainly the only time I've ridden it with people in suits.

In 2017 I was asked to go to Ontario in Canada to shoot a documentary about living a life devoted to off-road motorcycling. The producers of the film had chosen a cross-section of five riders to interview: Jamie Baskerville, aged fifteen, who is a GNCC racer; twenty-five-year-old Colton Haaker, who also rides for Husqvarna and is a former World SuperEnduro champion; Paul Rodden, aged seventy-five, who has been competing in Trials for over fifty years; and Larry Murray, who is sixty-five and is a former Can-Am and Husqvarna Enduro rider. And me, of course.

The producers filmed us riding together, but the main part of the documentary is the interviews they did, which were done separately, in pairs, such as me and Colton, and Larry and Paul, and then all of us together. It was all to do with finding out what makes an off-road motorcyclist tick, and it's worth checking out if you get time. It's called *Checkpoints* and is freely available on YouTube.

The reason I'm mentioning it here is because part of the documentary fits perfectly into the 'new experiences' category. While the producers were filming Paul and me having a chat, the beers started to flow, and if you ask anybody who knows me how many beers it takes to get me pissed they'll probably say one. I'm the original cheap date! The conversation gradually started to deteriorate, until we ended talking about condom catheters! Paul suggested that that's what they use in North America to solve the peeing problem during a race to which I replied that in Europe we just piss ourselves, which we usually do. The lowest point of the chat – or the highest point, depending on your sense of humour – is when Paul says that he wouldn't like to use any of my equipment, presumably meaning my trousers. 'Surely people would pay more for soiled pants,' I reply. We then go on to discuss the possibility of me starting my own condom catheter range called the G-Force Condom Catheter and Paul being my ambassador. It's all highbrow stuff!

A lot of people ask me how long I can carry on riding Hard Enduro, and to be honest I have no idea. I've recently signed a new two-year contract with Husqvarna, who I've been with for a while now, and if I see the contract through to the end, which I fully intend to, I'll be forty-five years of age. Incidentally, as an indication of how quickly Hard Enduro is growing, until recently Husqvarna used to send their big race truck to normal Enduro races, whereas now it tends to come with us.

In January 2019 I won the Tough One again, which was extremely gratifying. What made that particular win even sweeter was the fact that they'd changed it to a sprint – and, as any professional Hard Enduro rider will tell you, Graham Jarvis isn't supposed to win sprints. I'm seen as being Hard Enduro's Captain Slow and tend to make my time up on the hard stuff. The format was fastest speed over nine separate laps, and at the end they just divided your total time by nine to get your average. The display timer had been down during the race, so nobody knew the results until well after the race had ended. Because of my reputation, the last name the other riders were expecting to be called out was Jarvis, and to be honest I was thinking the same. Then again, if I was that slow on the fast sections, I wouldn't win anything, so perhaps it's just a perception that goes with my age. Graham's older than most of us, so he must be slow. Anyway, when they finally called my name out everybody just looked at each other and then looked at me in amazement! I felt slightly embarrassed at the time, so it wasn't difficult preventing myself from looking smug.

Something similar happened at the Hixpania in 2017. That one's quite a new race that has been going only about three years. It's already massive, though, in terms of popularity, and also has a Le Mans-style start, with the riders having to run into a cave to retrieve their bikes. It's done over three days and is judged on quite a complicated points system.

On the first day, which was the prologue, I didn't score any points at all, and by the end of the third day the organisers had decided that it was down to about three or four riders. Because of my performance on the first day, I was sure I wasn't one of them, so when the organisers finally called my name out as having tied for first place, I almost fainted. That wasn't all. I ended up being declared the winner because I'd won the last day. I remember it went very, very quiet when that happened, as the Spanish contingent had obviously been hoping for a home win, and the last person anybody had been expecting to walk away with the winner's trophy was me.

The rider who tied with me was Jonny Walker, and as far as I can remember he only had to finish third to secure the win. Unfortunately – for Jonny, at least, but not for me – on the very last hill he collided with a marshal and the two of them ended up rolling to the bottom. Jonny wasn't too happy, but then neither was the marshal. In subsequent years it became what's called a 'no help' zone. You have quite a few of those in Hard Enduro these days, and as time goes on I only expect them to increase.

I have a habit of springing surprises on people like that – or at least I have a habit of being the subject of these surprises.

A couple of weeks later I almost refuted this claim by doing the same thing again in France, which made my record for sprints in 2019 two out of two. I'll settle for that.

As long as I'm competitive and enjoying myself, I may as well keep riding Hard Enduro professionally. I'm not saying it doesn't get any harder, and as the sport becomes more popular you've got more and more good riders coming through, which is absolutely fantastic. I've never known there to be so much competition.

The two biggest threats to my career are a bit of back trouble, which I'll come on to in a second, and the aforementioned Jonny Walker. Apart from us both riding in Hard Enduro, Jonny and I have two things in common. First, we both come from a Trials background. As well as being a two-time British schoolboy champion, Jonny maintained a top ranking in Britain until he was seventeen. He also became the youngest ever recipient of the coveted Pinhard Prize, which is awarded to the highest achievers in motorsport under the age of twenty-one. Despite there being a sixteen-year gap between us, Jonny won the Pinhard just four years after I won it in 1996 when he was only nine and he too won it for Trials. He also competed twice at the European championships, in which I was once runner-up, so he was obviously no slouch when it came to Trials.

The second similarity is that we've both been lucky enough to have mentors who have been pivotal to our success. The only difference is that Jonny's mentor, Julian Stevens, who was also instrumental in bringing Knighter through, not to mention the four-time world Enduro champion Paul Edmondson, only came on the scene once Jonny had moved to Enduro, whereas Malcolm was obviously around in my Trials days. I think we were a similar age, though, when we met our mentors so the timing's about the same.

Like me, Jonny's head was eventually turned from Trials, and after competing in Enduro for a while he eventually found his home in Hard Enduro. Had Jonny stayed in Trials he could well have become another Dougie Lampkin, but fortunately for us he made the switch.

When I started coming through the ranks in our sport, the big star was obviously Taddy, and when I started winning things, which is when Taddy went over to eurocross, I took over his mantle. Then, just as I was beginning to dominate the sport, along came young Mr Walker, and we've been pushing each other ever since. In 2012, for instance, I won everything on the Hard Enduro calendar except the Erzberg. I won Romaniacs, the Tough One, Sea to Sky, Roof of Africa and Hell's Gate. Then, in 2013, I won all six – the Grand Slam of Hard Enduro. When that happened, I was on top of the world and it's undoubtedly the pinnacle of my career so far. Just five years earlier I'd been on the brink of calling it a day as a professional Trials rider and was all set for a second career flipping burgers.

Despite being anything but complacent about winning the Grand Slam, I was naturally hoping that something similar would happen the following year. Unluckily for me, that was Jonny's breakthrough year, and instead of Graham Jarvis winning the majority of the races, which had probably been expected, Jonny won everything except the Red Bull Sea to Sky. That was the only title I managed to retain, and as well as his emergence giving me a bit of a kick up the arse it created even more interest in the sport. Since then, as far as Jonny and me are concerned, it's been six of one and half a dozen of the other, and thanks to the likes of Billy Bolt, Wade Young, Alfredo Gómez, Cody Webb, Manny Lettenbichler and Mario Roman – to name but a few – things have opened up even more in recent years, and there are several of us now who are all capable of winning the big races.

In the past, I've actually taught Alfredo, Mario *and* Jonny during my schooling career. Apparently, Alfredo and Mario came to a Trials school I ran in Madrid once, but I don't remember them. With Jonny it was slightly different, as his dad had paid me to take him out for a lesson. He too was with Malcolm's team at the time and was riding as a schoolboy. He had a bit of promise, I suppose, but I remember thinking to myself at the time that he was nothing special. How he's proved me wrong!

With regards to the backache, well, that's just wear and tear really. It's been niggling me since my Trials days and is never going to get better. It's what happens when you get to my age, and although I doubt that backache alone will be responsible for my eventual retirement, it may well be a contributing factor. Even as far back as 2013 I was being called a freak of nature by the press, because nobody could understand how I was able to carry on riding and winning Hard Enduro races. They didn't mean it disrespectfully. They just couldn't get their heads around it. These days I think the novelty has worn off a bit, and although people occasionally take the piss out of me for being an old man, they tend to spend more time asking me how I do slow wheelies or win races than how I get out of bed in the morning or when I'll be getting my bus pass.

The person I see most at races is obviously Damo, my mechanic. He's employed by Husqvarna and is basically my partner-in-crime. He's from Rochdale originally, so the wrong side of the Pennines, but he's a good lad, and he can actually ride a motorbike pretty well. In fact, Damo claims that years ago he won tickets to one of my Trials schools but found it so boring that he pretended his bike had broken so he could go home early! To soften the blow, he says he wasn't into Trials much which is why he found it boring. That's alright then! Whenever Damo has a bad result on his bike I always say to him afterwards that had he bothered to stay on at the Jarvis School of Motorcycling, he would probably have fared better. I won't say what he says in return.

As well as being in charge of all things mechanical, Damo's the person who has to deal with my own reactions after winning or losing a race. To be fair, that's probably one of the easiest parts of his job, as nobody's ever been able to tell the difference.

One of the best things about Damo is that nothing fazes him. What's more, he calls a spade a spade. Some young mechanics might have become a bit overwhelmed by working for a big factory team, but Damo couldn't give a monkey's. It's a job, but one he does very well. He's very confident, and because things don't faze him, it's always quiet and calm around him. If Damo thinks somebody's a prick, he'll say so, regardless of who they are. He's got more stories than you can wave a stick at. Whether all of them are true or not, I couldn't say, but they're all entertaining!

We did almost go our separate ways once. About four years ago we were in Ales in France – or at least I was – and after checking into the hotel I got an early night. For some reason Damo was arriving separately to me, and when he did, he checked in to the hotel. Nobody had told us this, but whoever booked the rooms had decided to put us together, and when he entered the room, it was like a herd of bloody elephants had come in. I'd been fast asleep at the time, but I wasn't now. I was wide awake!

Damo's only words to me were, 'Don't wake me up in the morning', which he said before turning off the lights. He had to be joking.

By this time I was spitting bloody feathers and instead of putting my head back on the pillow like I should have I got up and started slamming doors and saying lots of rude words under my breath. I ended up breaking the handle on the bathroom door, and after a brief exchange of words Damo got in his van and went to find another hotel. To be fair, he'd just driven hundreds of miles, and I had a bad back, so I think we were both a bit grumpy. Since then we've never shared a room again – or are ever likely to! It's the only time we've ever fallen out. He's a really good lad, is Damo, and very, very good at his job. I'm lucky to have him.

I think the only person who spends any amount of time wondering about my retirement now, apart from Sandra who is probably dreading me being under her feet, is me, and that's only because I have to. The closest I've come to making any plans is getting a house in Spain, from where I've recently started operating residential riding schools. Is this an advert? I suppose it is really.

Over the last few years I've been doing more and more schools, and although I could never see myself doing them full-time, they're a great way to earn a few quid in between races. They've even helped me to come out of my shell a bit. The person who first suggested I start doing them was a friend of mine called John Kerwin. John organises Enduro events and designs courses, and one day he asked me if I'd like to do a training school for him. I'd only just started riding Enduro, so in addition to wondering whether anyone would turn up I wasn't sure I'd be up to it. In the end people did, thank God, and I somehow managed to blag it. One of the things that got me through the school was that a lot of the riders just wanted to learn Trials skills, so it ended up being a Trials lesson on Enduro bikes. It was at that point I realised that I knew enough about Trials – and would soon know enough about Enduro – to be able to do this sort of thing on a regular basis, and it just went on from there.

I haven't always been keen on teaching, though, which probably won't surprise you. Malcolm and Rhoda used to run a course for young riders, and while I was living with them they once asked me to come in and answer a few questions. Being shy, I obviously wasn't too keen, but I obliged all the same.

When I first went to Malcolm and Rhoda, I used to find it difficult separating the different sections at a Trial in my head, and that's one of the first things Malcolm and I worked on. I'd ride up to a section, five it, as in get five points, get very angry and then ride up and five the next one, and so it went on. Malcolm taught me how to block out what had happened at the previous section and treat each one individually, and when he spoke to me in front of these youngsters, that's what he asked me about. Rhoda reminded me of this story the other day, and it made me wonder how on earth I ended up doing schools in the first place.

'How did you get over fiving every section, Graham?' Malcolm asked. He was obviously expecting me to say something insightful and inspirational.

'I just stopped caring,' I said quietly.

'What?' The look on Malcolm's face was a picture. Pure shock!

'That's not what you were supposed to say, Graham', he said.

'Really? Oh, sorry. I'll be off then.'

As part of my training, Malcolm had told me not to care about what had gone on before, so I was just repeating what I'd learned. I think it was my delivery that spoiled it.

With regards to my shyness, deciding to run schools was a baptism of fire. Before I got the place in Spain, I'd get on a plane bound for America or Mexico or somewhere and then spend four or five days with ten or twenty complete strangers who were all expecting me to communicate with them and teach them how to ride.

The thing is, it's my job to make the people I'm teaching feel at ease, not the other way around. Being in that situation changed everything for me, as all of a sudden I was worrying about them instead of worrying about myself. I can also spot shy or nervous people a mile away, so if I spot one during a school, I'll always make a special effort to make them feel at ease.

The only time I get a bit tongue-tied is when somebody is nervous about meeting me, because that just makes me nervous! It doesn't happen all that often, but when it does the two of us stand there like lemons for a few seconds until I remember that I'm supposed to be making them feel at ease. If people ever acted like that in front of me twenty years ago, or said something complimentary, I'd just smile and walk away, for the simple reason I didn't know how to handle it. One of the most regrettable things about me being shy is that it's often been mistaken for either ignorance or arrogance, but that couldn't be further from the truth. Nobody decides to be terminally shy. It's something you're born with. Without wanting to sound too dramatic, it's definitely damaged my career, and if I could have changed it, I would. One-to-one I wasn't too bad once I got to know somebody, but that could take time and unfortunately some people would give up on me. Malcolm often retells the story about a time that he and I drove to Poland and apparently I only said three words to him and two of those were yes. I was obviously in a world of my own.

These days if somebody says something nice to me, I love it. I haven't turned into Mr Chatty or anything, so I don't talk them to death afterwards, but I'll make sure they know that I appreciate being appreciated. That's the most important thing.

I still run schools in different countries today – all over

the world, in fact – but these days it's a heck of a lot easier. Funnily enough, the vast majority of people I now teach have no idea about my background in Trials, and as far as they're concerned I've been riding Hard Enduro from the off. When I first tell them, they're often surprised, but when I tell them how instrumental it's been in my progression in Hard Enduro, they become interested.

Something else that John Kerwin has persuaded me to have a go at – and this is taking up more and more of my time these days – is designing courses for Trials and Hard Enduro, something I hadn't done since helping out Brian Dobin in the woods behind our house. When it comes to Hard Enduro courses, I've got a bit of a reputation as a designer. After a practice session at a race in Barnsley one year on a course that I'd designed, some of the riders complained that it was tougher than the Erzberg! I'm not sure about that, but I certainly enjoyed designing it.

Taddy Błażusiak has recently started his own race in Poland called the 111 Megawatt, and although I haven't won it – yet – I have competed in it once or twice. It takes place in Europe's largest coal mine, which is in Belchatów, Poland, and it attracts a massive number of spectators. Maybe I'll do something similar one day?

That really is one of the best things about Hard Enduro – the locations – and it's another reason I keep on competing. Just take a look at my Instagram or my Facebook accounts. They're like travel brochures!

My first opportunity to design a Trials course was for a new World Trial round that John was organising up in Cumbria. When it comes to designing courses, John's more of an Enduro man and he asked me if I'd be interested. To design and build a course for a round of the outdoor world championship was obviously a big challenge, but I snatched his hand off. The first one I constructed was on an Enduro course in Cumbria. After receiving some very positive feedback from the riders, the teams and the FIM, we were asked to do it again the following year. The last course I designed for a world championship round was in 2016 in Tong in Yorkshire. I made sure there were plenty of muddy banks on the sections, so if I'd taken part, I might have done quite well. Then again . . .

Because I'd designed the courses and had helped organise these events, I obviously attended them as well, and each time I went at least a hundred people would ask me if I missed riding Trials. I think they were hoping I'd say yes, but I had to tell the truth and say, 'No, I'm afraid I don't.' I like attending Trials as a spectator, and have enjoyed designing sections, but that's as far as it goes for me. Things have progressed so much in Trials since I was competing, and when I look at some of the things that the current Trials world champion Toni Bou manages to do, I'm left scratching my head. The only thing I'd consider coming out of retirement for is the Scott Trial. It was suggested a couple of years ago that I ride it using my Husqvarna 300TE, and I like the sound of that. Maybe I will give it a go one day.

Somebody asked me the other day if I'd ever tried any acting before. Then, once they'd got to know me a bit, they retracted the question on the grounds that I might have to speak occasionally. In all seriousness, doing television is something I quite enjoy, and over the last few years I've been asked to make one or two appearances – with my helmet on! One of the most bizarre experiences I've had in front of the television cameras was when I was asked to appear on the American version of *Top Gear* (not to be confused with its replacement, *Top Gear America*), which ran from 2010 until 2016. One of the show's presenters was the rally driver Tanner Foust, and I was asked by somebody if I'd like to race him up in Scotland. I'd be riding my Husqvarna 300TE that I use today and Tanner would be driving a buggy. It sounded like a bit of a laugh, so I said yes, why not.

I'd been watching *Top Gear* for donkey's years, and I'd always wondered whether the races they put on were fixed or not. Given the fact that they always went down to the wire I figured they probably were, but I had no idea to what extent. When I arrived in Scotland, we got straight on with the filming, and the first thing the director said to me and Tanner confirmed my worst suspicions. 'Right then,' he said. 'We're going to film the ending first. Is that OK? It's going to be close, but Tanner's going to win.' I couldn't believe it! Hope I haven't shattered anybody's illusions.

To make it look like a real race, they filmed each section in a different location, but to save time they filmed two of the sections in the same location but with Tanner and me going in opposite directions. It was like WWF on wheels, really. Entertaining, but ultimately a pantomime.

The only other thing I've thought about with regards to my future is the possibility of running my own team or becoming a team manager. The idea of passing my knowledge and experience on to younger riders, just as Malcolm has done, is something that's becoming increasingly important to me, which is another reason I enjoy doing the schools. Whether or not it will happen is anyone's guess, but the more I think about the idea the more I like it.

As far as almost every aspect of my career goes – my progression in Trials and eventual success, crossing to Enduro, and even schools and ideas about team management – all roads seem to lead back to the aforementioned Mr Malcolm Rathmell, so he's the person I'd like to pay a final tribute to.

I think I said earlier that I must have been a very frustrating pupil for Malcolm, and if he hadn't stuck with me like he did, and hadn't devoted so much time and effort to helping me, I wouldn't be where I am today. A good way to demonstrate the enormity of Malcolm's efforts is to compare our relationship with the relationship between Mart and Dougie. It was Rhoda who suggested this to me, and it's an excellent observation.

Mart used to instruct Dougie, whereas Malcolm used to have to bring me around and coax it out of me. Also, Dougie was Mart's son, which meant Mart could, within reason, say anything he wanted. Malcolm obviously had to tread differently with me, and he did that brilliantly. I must have been hard work, though.

Whether I could ever have been world champion will always be open to debate, but one thing's for sure: the fact that I never made it had nothing to do with Malcolm and everything to do with me. If it hadn't been for him, it's doubtful I'd have won the Scott Trial, and if I hadn't won the Scott, I might never have fallen into Hard Enduro. There are, of course, a million and one other reasons why Malcolm Rathmell has been important to my career, but that's probably the main one, as after twenty years of trying I finally became the best in my field. It might have happened a bit late in life, but we're patient, Malcolm and me. The main thing is that with his help, I got there.

Thanks, Malcolm.

PICTURE CREDITS

The author and publisher are grateful to the following for permission to reproduce the following photographs:

Section 1
Derek Stingemore: p.1 (below), p.5 (above)
John Hulme: p.2 (below), p.7 (above and below), p.8 (above and below)
Colin Bullock: p.6 (below)

Section 2
John Hulme: p. 9 (above and below), p. 10 (above)
HusqvarnaFuture7Media: p.10 (below), p.11 (above and below), p.12 (above and below), p.13 (above and below), p.14 (above and below), p.15 (above and below), p.16